Cover Image: Pilatus Porter on the Ruth Glacier,
Mt McKinley. DeHavilland Beaver in background

Last of the Long Hunters
Hunting the Alaskan Frontier by Air—the last years
By Mark Rose

Genesis Alive LLC 2015©
www.genesisalive.com

Mark D. Rose July, 2015
ISBN: 978-0-9960665-2-5
ISBN: 978-0-9960665-3-2 Digital Versions

For Pat

Contents

Introduction

Last of the Long Hunters relates the experiences of an aviator working in the Alaskan Arctic. The story is not untypical of those who flew that wild backcountry in the post WWII era. The events recoded are to promote a better understanding of this period and as a tribute to those who blazed these wilderness trails by *air,* they as a whole contributing to the development of the State in innumerable ways.

The account occurs during the period prior to the dispersal of Alaska lands into parks and native land withdrawals in the 1980s. As a result of these Federal actions, free access and hunting privileges to these immense tracts of territory were lost forever, this in the name of "preservation and the public good" during the Carter administration. These acts were imposed over the objections of many Alaskans, as in essence much of the country would be locked up from then on, and the flying long hunter era would end.

Few roads exist across those expanses even today, excepting those tracts close to civilization in the lower quarter of the State. The lion's share of the country remains unseen by most of the populace to this day, excepting the local village populations and the wealthy; those who can afford to tour the immense "parks" - maintained at great pubic expense for the benefit of a few, mostly the rangers themselves.

In those early years the vistas of Mt McKinley and furthest north Fairbanks were merely jump-off points for this group of hardy adventurers, a place to fuel up and go as they struck *north*.

Alaska is a place like no other on Earth; her broad rivers bound by countless precipices; rugged coast lines jutting into wild Pacific surf, and her boundless plains prolific with freely roaming wildlife. These expanses measured in hundreds of thousands of square *miles*, not merely acres. Her varied climates and violent storms are well known, threatening the stoutest ships and stranding many a traveler to their peril in the interior. The sum of this varied geography coming together—towering mountains, plains, glaciers, rivers, lakes and streams—are unequaled on Earth, creating breathtaking scenes of grandeur incapable of written description and mocking the lens of the best camera.

To this place men came in the early days, first to find fur and gold; then to fight a World War. At the conclusion of the latter more of adventuresome spirit were added to the population, their heart and souls feeling the call to explore and search out every inch of her magnificence and build a new life within her borders. These efforts were aptly rewarded in 1959, with the Alaska Territory winning Statehood and the 49th star was added to the flag of the United States.

In the natural course of time came those coveted institutions of justice, government and family that make a true society. In 1900, the Honorable Judge George Wickersham was assigned the Federal bench of the central territory of 500,000 square miles, named Alaska District Number Two, the magistrate a hearty man of firm constitution and purpose. A fine traveler, the Judge and wife were well suited to the daunting task the country placed before them. Wickersham, a citizen of Washington State, was appointment by President McKinley to this important bench. Recommended to the post by a number of upstanding citizens who had stake in the great territory; these forward thinking citizens seeing the benefit a Federal Court would bring to this remote Territory in the course of Empire.

Traveling by ship to Skagway and onto the Yukon gold fields by foot, Yukon City in particular; it happened the good Judge arrived just late for an organic service of matrimony in those parts, but not an affair completely by mutual consent. Apparently some Dapper Dan had jilted one Jill so to speak, a well loved yet innocent damsel of the dance floor in this frontier town. Angered by this gent's dishonorable conduct and attempt to flee the country for better parts, a posse formed and captured the guilty scoundrel, just before he made good his escape. Forming a court and fixing a *rope* as incentive for the gents consideration, after a short deliberation (which included the testimony of the defrocked); a judgment of *guilty* was decreed and sentence was reached; the *alter or the tree*. Now Dan, after a moment to consider his options, wisely chose the former. With this "confession" a happy ceremony of matrimony ensued (by this same court) and instantly the mood of the mob reversed. Hence a great celebration ensued, the couple now amazingly reconciled. (Noting in the record a $500 bail was ordered to be paid by the perpetrator, this posted for birthing fees if so required). At the conclusion of this affair, it was noted a great volume of spirits were consumed; this in honor of the happy occasion said to have completely depleted the available stock for miles around.

His Honor was early called on to conduct that sacred service summer or winter, by dogsled or river, gold strike or trail, following the miner parties across the interior and helping establish an orderly society and governance, the foundation of *Nation*. It should be noted that a tax was also established by the Judgeship upon entrance to the country, this as monetary support for the new Judicial District as directed by Washington. Such income was obtained by authorizing a $1,000 liquor license levied on the *Saloons,* a profitable business in those parts.[1]

Many from the continent found good wives from among the native inhabitants, others coming north with their spouses; and soon more of that gender arrived in support of the War effort. Thusly, by and by the foundations of Nation came to be, a *Great State* forming, grounding the hearts and minds of good people both native and white, refined in the crucible of this country, developing a class of sturdy men and women who persevered in this Last Frontier.

---

[1] *Old Yukon, Trails, Trials and Tales*, Judge J. Wickersham 1937 See also *History of Alaska* Bancroft, 1895

1

Jed Smith, circa 1925

The First *Long Hunters*

In American History, the first Long Hunters struck out from the Eastern settlements with muzzle loader, knife and knapsack, heading for the sacred Indian lands of the Tennessee and Kentucky territories, ancestral hunting grounds of the Cherokee, Shawnee and other tribes. Though brimming with game and perfect for settlement, a "dark and bloody land" the natives called *it*, so hotly contested between tribes none dared settle that country. At sight, opposing bands would enter into an instant and vicious battle, no more than tolerate a white skin in thieir country. Dauntless, *Long Hunters* such as Daniel Boone, Davy Crocket and others defied these dangers and established outposts, these meager settlements becoming towns, then cities. So by sheer will, determination and the ever assisting hand of *Providence,* civilized man eventually settled the country, but not without terrible loss, setback and hardship.

The deeds of Lewis and Clark are well enough known, but others came and actually stayed on and lived in the country; trappers like Jedediah Smith,[2] Kit Carson and Joe Meek[3] possessing the Rocky Mountains and westward, yet despite discouragement, loss and terrible hardships they held on, homesteading the country ahead of the great wagon trains of the mid-1840s. These such as Joe Meek in particular in Oregon, becoming the West's first Sherriff. It was these who married and truly settled the country, Carson a Southwestern General, but Smith meeting an untimely end at the hand of the Comanche's while searching for water on the Santé Fe in 1832. Jed left the Oregon Territory only after shaking hands with Hudson Bay Chief Proctor McLaughlin at Ft. Vancouver in 1825, (shortly after his band was massacred on the Oregon coast, he and a handful of survivors fleeing to the fort). Arriving naked and without weapons that same year, Smith left the country the following under mutual agreement heading eastbound, carrying with him the first map of the Oregon Trail. This document included the location of the critical South Pass route east of modern Cody, WY, the only known passage allowing wagons to pass for 500 miles. Once the

---

[2] *Jedediah Smith and the Opening of the West,* Dale Morgan 1956
[3] *Kit Carson Days,* Sabin 1914

2

Whitman's and Spalding's brought wagons through this same pass in 1838, (missionaries coming at the 1832 request of the western natives, see note 3) and as word got out that carriage could be brought west, the immigration to Oregon began. None can deny these men the due they deserve as frontiersmen and pathfinders, all true American Patriots and *Long Hunters* to a man.

2

Reeve's Fairchild in Valdez, Alaska, circa 1935

The Pioneers

On March 30, 1867 Alaska was purchased from Russia, no less important an event then the Louisiana, California or the Southwest acquisitions in 1847 before, adding this strategic and immense archipelago to our Union. The Russians, their fur trade now exhausted and in need of war funds, (and mistakenly thinking the tract useless, save for some fish and lumber) turns out made a grievous error, as gold was soon discovered in equally immense quantities as California, eventually fostering the rush of '98 that engulfed the entire Yukon and Alaska

Territory. In like frustration to the Russian Czar, so was the King of Spain: (who lost California to the *Forty-Niner's*) both unknowingly sitting upon their ever coveted pots of gold, now handed on the cheap to the Americans! As it happened in Alaska, the chief city of the former Russian possession being Sitka, this only a short distance west of a quiet native habitation on the mainland, this where the coveted metal was found in immense quantities! Gold being discovered in that place after the transfer to America by one *Joseph Juneau* in 1880, the city namesake of the world's most productive gold mine for more than a decade to come! Who can deny that Providence decided that both the gold and country was to be American in both cases!

Still unsatisfied, that great American spirit of exploration and commerce marched on in the minds of the miners from the Juneau lode, who now "grubstaked" (outfitted) and thrust out in all directions, including north, blowing open the Yukon strikes and many more in the coming years. Sprinting across Alaska making one discovery after another; now in Circle City then in Fairbanks, they didn't stop until they were on the Arctic coast at Nome only two years later in 1900! At this rate had not the Russian border and Bering's Sea hindered them, the Czar would have met this industrious lot at the gates of Petersburg the following summer. Such are the freedoms established by our wise forefathers; this in contrast to the corrupt serfdoms they forsook in Europe to form the new world. Free commerce and the American way had again won the day, and Alaska was here to stay.

In such spirit these came to the Great Land, seeking adventure, exploration, and inventive commerce. Alaska now going through a transformation; this as these inventive and industrious minds, armed with the hope of the American Dream pressed onward. Understand miners and mines need supplies like no other industry: find a productive mine and civilization will soon follow. But this new frontier presented obstacles requiring herculean efforts to move about and resupply. Water being the only reliable mode of transport in those times, and for lack of road, they spread out across the basins and tributaries as best they could, and soon the Yukon River itself became the backbone of commerce in the state by boat, the mountain ranges too massive and plains impassable for wagon or horseback. The problem due to the soft muck and hummocks referred to as "muskeg" in this country, passable only by the moose or caribou and not the domestic beast pulling a cart. Only in winter could the dogsled move across these barriers, these pups limited in range and by the extreme weather plus food supply, the distances being exceeding great to fully transit the territory.

Tons of equipment and stores were needed by the miners, leaving only the hardiest outdoorsmen or native to strike out into the depths of the country adjacent to the Yukon, Tanana, Chena, Copper or Susitna Rivers, this in support of their claims.

So enters the single engine *airplane* into the theater, brought north by ship and assembled at ports like Seward, Valdez and Anchorage for such use. Enduring its quirks, shortcomings and a plethora of failures, these new machines were early utilized to push further and further into the unknown country, even to the tops of Glaciers (e.g. Reeve in Valdez). Operational limits of these early craft were often exceeded and beyond, engine failure the common plague of them all. Crew's fortunate enough to escape with their lives often ended their career in total loss or bankruptcy. Further, no formal maps existed, save what the pilots held in memory or personally hand printed. Later on, aerial photos helped these trailblazers find their destination and return, if the weather was clear enough to compare the images to ground formations along their path. (The pilot carrying a stack of photos on his knee, hoping he had them in order and careful to not let them blow out in the slip-stream.)

Though there were earlier flights in Alaska with experimental biplanes, most acknowledge Fairbanks businessman James Martin be named among the first to bring a commercially produced single engine craft to the Alaskan Interior with commercial ambitions. His plane, the 1912 single seat Gage-Martin Tractor Plane, shipped by sea to Skagway. She then loaded on the famous White Pass Railroad and sent to Whitehorse, Yukon Territory, then on to Fairbanks via riverboat on the Yukon, Tanana and finally the Chena rivers, arriving in at that place June 21, 1913. After several sobering fights hoping to generate airshow ticket sales, Martin abandoned the flying business, shipping his Gage Martin south to San Francisco to be sold. But Alaska now had a taste of aviation, and more would have their try.

Later in 1920, General Billy Mitchell came up with an idea for an official flight from New York to Nome, this in hopes to gain public attention and funding for his fledging Airforce, recently returned from operations in the French theater of war. Picking the powerful De Havilland DH-4B aircraft, these fitted with a new 400 Horsepower 12 cylinder "Liberty" engine, the expedition date was set, led by one Lt. St. Clair Streett, the wing named the "Black Wolf" Squadron.[4]

A "Black Wolf" squadron US Army De Havilland,
Fairbanks, Circa 1920

Leaving Mitchell Field on Long Island July 5, 1920, the flight of four specially equipped planes set off Northeast. By August 14th, they all landed successfully near Wrangell, Alaska at Sergief Island, breaking a number of records in the process. They appeared over the Capitol at Juneau August 16 and 17th respectively in pairs, the first dropping a special parcel for then Governor Riggs. Though hampered by mechanical problems and weather, all four assembled in Fairbanks by August 23rd, the first pair arriving safely at that city on the 19th. This all an amazing feat for cross-country aviation and Alaska.

Then on August 23rd, the full wing made the final dash to Nome via Ruby, and after successfully negotiating several squalls blocking their direct route arrived at their

---

[4] *See Alaskan Aviation History* Vol. 1, Robert W. Stevens 1990

ultimate objective Nome on Monday, August 23, 1920 at 3:05 PM, landing at the field prepared at Fort Davis, this to

First airplane over Juneau, Alaska, August 16th 1920

a cheering crowd of hundreds being congratulated by the base Commander, Capt. Douglas.

They had flown a mere 55 hours covering the 4500 mile stretch from Long Island to Nome. Upon return, the squadron chocked up a round trip total time of 110 hours in the air, returning to Mitchell Field by October 8. The round trip distance traveled of approximately 8,700 miles.

Others soon followed, Alaska now on the hearts and minds of these aviation minded pioneers forever. Other notables who followed were found in Ben Eielson and Noel Wien, these making the push to Pt. Barrow in March of 1927, but not without costing one plane lost to the Arctic ice and one left grounded in the process, one member losing his fingers to frost bite, caused by the 80 mile trek off the ice from their abandoned craft. Being forced down by fuel exhaustion and an unscheduled emergency landing, (which cost them precious daylight and fuel), rescue efforts to locate them failing. However, much was learned on the expedition, the fuel stash method successfully employed, as even with modifications no plane had the fuel capacity to make it out and back to Barrow for a round trip, aviation fuel could not to be found anywhere lest you carried it along yourself. So in the end the score was Arctic 2, man 1, a game that goes on to this day.

Eielson and Wien's Stinson at Fairbanks with crated 2x5 gallon fuel tins, ready to load up and set the first stash in the Arctic, Circa 1927

Now as these expanses became better known, in the course of time and a World War many of these challenges were overcome, the forerunners literally crashing their way into the country and again, at a terrible cost to men and machine.

Not content lest the *whole country* be mapped and touched they pushed on, using every improvisation and wit so commonly known to the American way. Finally, most of the blank areas on the maps were filled, but not all. In the course of time through experiment, effort and skill, safer and more reliable airborne equipment began to appear in the State, allowing the dream to become reality. Now these men had the equipment able to unravel the uncharted Alaskan Interior, previously known only through the verbal traditions of the Natives and the meager notes of a few intrepid adventurers. Even with these vastly improved and reliable flying machines that came into use in the late 1930s, a surprisingly high toll was still paid, as accidents continued to plague these endeavors in the processes of advancement and discovery. In truth, the story of challenge and adventure has not ceased today, continuing even at this writ, the harsh realities of terrain and weather exacting their annual toll upon man and machine year after year, the reality being this: *no matter how much technology and effort is thrown at the country, it remains stubborn and undefeated,* humbling the best pilots and most advanced equipment every year.

The Super Cub

In those days almost no wired or wireless communications existed across the expanses, especially from air to ground, the distance an area equivalent to 2/3 of the entire "lower 48" States combined. Planning had to be perfect and include alternative actions (there being little or no means of making a call for assistance if accident, mishap or sudden storm came) adding to the challenge faced by these early aviators.

Though the obstacles were great, we should not be surprised to find a breed of men who stood out unique and fearless, up to the challenge and unsatisfied of being shackled to the road or water-bound courses, yearning to explore the unseen expanses of that great untouched *Alaskan Interior*. Many of these fellows were veterans of the aforementioned World War and well trained in various crafts, including the handling of a rifle and controls of an aircraft. Now independent of roads, boat or dogsled, many a winter evening was spent with maps spread out in lamplight, trekking across the territory on paper—planning, calculating and preparing to enter these trackless expanses. The thought of seeing the unseen, hunting the un-hunted, and panning the un-panned drove them on, they now employing a new mode of transport, such as the "Norseman," "Fairchild" "Beaver," "Cessna," "Stintsman" and of course the dauntless "Cub." These capable of crossing distances that formerly took months in *hours*. The out country or "Bush" as it was called, where greats like Wien, Gillam, Dickson, Crossman, Merrill and Reeve were made, the country now becoming civilized routes for mail and commerce. But alas, travel into the trackless and uninhabited *Arctic* was generally unneeded and often unwanted. Nothing was out there to be named civilization they said, yet *frontier* still existed in the hundreds of thousands of square *miles* there, untouched and unseen by civilized man. This is what drew them you understand, they had to see, touch and search it all out - every last unmapped mountain, valley, river, creek and plain; not to mention the game the country contained— an immense quantity of that.

The most troublesome issue in the early days was engine failure, Bob Reeve alone having 13 in just one aircraft you see, his last forcing a bay-water landing on snow skis. Grateful his craft halted upright, Bob thinking himself safe and in the tidal shallows, stepped off his airless steed to find he had landed atop a tide covered boulder, and dunked immediately over his head in Valdeze bay! Now this chilly dip finally convinced the pilot-turned-swimmer it was time for a plane change. The perplexing issue of that day being what aircraft to choose, as *all* the motor options of that time were potentially a deadly step *backward*. Bob must have made the right choice; he flew on to found the successful *Reeve Aleutian Airways,* finally picking the 4 motor turbine-powered Lockheed Electra in the end. Of course why pick a warm route to Tahiti when you could fly the worst weather in the world to *Attu!* That was Bob Reeve[5] for you, Alaska and flying was in his blood for good.

---

[5] *Glacier Pilot* - The Story of Bob Reeve, Day 1957

3

The Deep Interior, 70⁰ North

In the far interior, there were no spares, fuel or landing strips, so if one became disabled, your craft could sit for *years,* no matter how minor the issue, something as simple as your engine failing to start finishing the deal. One could find himself weathered in till spring, unable to affect a rescue, as temperatures were capable of turning downward *100 degrees* overnight.[6] Dog sleds most often couldn't reach you, even if the locals knew your craft was

---

[6] The author personally experienced such in the Arctic fall of 1976

down. Across the North Slope in specific, only a handful of villages kept teams, such as Anaktuvuk, Wainwright, Pt. Lay and Barrow, this to cover an area of over 100,000 square miles with a range of less than 100 themselves. If taken to hike out, following a river course could literally lead *nowhere,* dumping into some desolate bay without any maritime connection at all. For example, one helicopter crew of the author's knowledge was forced down in the middle of the Brooks Range, unable to find a passage south forced to land for lack of fuel. After sitting for a week with starvation and cold threatening, and no sign of help on the way, they elected to hike out in minus 40 temperatures rather take a chance of dying in place. Fortunately, one of the party was adept to jumping into unfrozen river eddies, this in order to catch a few fish, which sustained the starving party. In order to survive the chilly dip, immediately upon exiting the water another of the party would quickly exchange clothing with the man, this in order to dry his garments by fire. And so it went for many days, the group finally arriving at that remote outpost of Umiat, thought to have perished in a mountain crash for certain by the searchers.[7]

If fortunate enough to luck into an inhabited bay, the locals would often consist of a few Eskimos who couldn't speak English; those habitations found along the coastal areas far from the interior. As previously stated, there were few means of communication in those times, the locals having only the capability of transporting the

---

[7] The Evergreen incident, circa 1960. The aircraft was later recovered but some of the 10 member crew suffered frostbite

downed flyers within range of dogsled or kayak; waiting for the seasonal trading ship or traders that came once an annum, at best dashing to a station where a wireless set could be found. It should be said that more than one downed flyer owed his life to these intrepid fellows of the north, who answered the call for help without hesitation, often at peril to their own lives. Accomplishing selfless feats of courage to affect rescue at all costs, these folk oft escaping with lives only to show for their effort. That was the law of the land, human life a precious commodity.

With little or no chance of recovering a disabled plane nor chance of getting word out, quite simply *no one* desired to fly out there, as the light aircraft capable of landing had not the fuel capacity to go and come, lest a system of fuel depots were established, called *stashes*. As mentioned, distances were too great for portable radios to operate until nearly 1940 and that a gamble; the country too immense to be found if forced down or crashed.

The first wireless set in Alaska designed for aircraft was used with success by Roy Dickson, circa 1937, who actually had one of these devices aboard new-in-the-box when his ski-equipped craft broke through the ice on a remote lake. Make-shifting the connections and antenna, Dickson transmitted in the blind for days as they watched their stores deplete, battery go dead and temperatures drop. As Providence would have it, one night the Coast Guard Clipper Haida was in on patrol range, the radioman scanning the frequency bands to fend off boredom, caught a transmission that included the parties coordinates. Many days later some tiny black objects appeared at the far end of the lake, thinking they now had wolves to contend with, the party was pleasantly surprised to hear signal gunfire and were promptly rescued. Afterward Dickson sent a letter off to one Bill Lear, owner of the radio manufacturer of the set, thanking him for the timely utility of this new device.[8]

There were no people or airstrips *anywhere* in that part of the territory, but unlike the Deserts of Sahara, the country was alive with game and habitual in the summer months; if you carried the right equipment and enough bug dope. It was this country the sketchy maps and blank charts were opened to, this country that dazzled the imagination of these forerunners.

Out there among those unnamed ribbons of water, mountain peaks, passes, canyons and lakes, satisfaction could be found you see, the indomitable spirit of adventure in its primal form fulfilled. Experiencing the sight of a hundred thousand caribou on the move transported the place back in time, likened to that of the Wild West 150 years before. Even cash income could be generated from the country, that if you were so lucky, a payback for your craft, fuel and supplies expended. This was *Frontier,* last on the American Continent and maybe the world, and this adventuresome group had no intention of being denied it. So they set out with resolve and paid a price they did, the place fit only for the *Long Hunters* and their new mode of transport—the single engine light aircraft.

Excellent at improvising, airfields were often self-built and kept secret, concealing a niche of country then accessed by foot or any other means that could fit inside or

[8] *Roy Dickson, 1930's Alaska Bush Pilot* Dickson Jr. and McLaren 2009 a must read on this early period

17

out of their planes; such to be reassembled on-site. Bush landing sites often consisted of sweeping gravel bars along the rivers or sometimes a flat hilltop—if you had the courage to try. More than a few left their craft as a memorial or expensive pile of tubing and rag in these places; marking the loss and the beginning of a many weeks ordeal, hoping for a chance to be rescued. Some were never heard from again nor their craft found. We only had their final waging wing or "see ya" to remember them back at the jump-off points. That was the way it was in this country.

We only knew it was over if the FAA dropped the search effort and/or the wreckage spotted. At this point every effort was made to execute a rescue and extract the party. If the worse was obvious you would roll out and set a compass heading for home, this with a heavy heart and sometime choked voice over the wireless, making effort not to show emotion. Sometimes we were surprised, like if someone would emerge a weeks later in the walkout, lucky to have been spotted in a place where an extraction could be pulled off. Such made the news for a week and talk in the hangar; but forgotten just as quickly and replaced by another—we all knowing it could be us next time.

Evidence of the lost were sometimes located decades later; this when their craft spilled out a glacier or was spotted on a windless day at the bottom of some remote lake, their end a mystery known only to the Almighty and the local game. If you survived and were spotted alive, further drops of supply were provided, the problem of extraction then sorted out by the government for us. Messages were dropped directing the downed party to a pickup location, a system of signals worked out, this also printed on the back of our hunting permits, accomplished by stamping out characters and/or made with dark branches in the snow for sight contrast. Assistance could also arrive in the form of a paratrooper/doctor, this system worked out in the war if such capable staff were available.

In time, man always finds a way. Recovery and rescue options improved dramatically when the *helicopters* showed up in the country, first as part of the Geophysical Year of 1955. In their infinite wisdom, the US Government sent 12 helicopters to fly and conquer in that day; and shortly after all 12 were destroyed in various mishaps. It took years before reliable and longer range rotor ships came on the scene to fill the gap, yet they were quickly and aptly deployed as soon as available. But like their fixed wing counterparts, their operational capability was pushed past design limits in this country, an environment no manufacturer could test for nor replicate. In these early years many sad endings occurred among the rotor-wing fleet, often with loss of life and machine, helicopters causing more fatalities per crash than fixed-wing aircraft, this due to the more vertical impact upon engine failure and the cockpit setup. Undaunted, the survivors continued and the heli's flew on, taking on a vital role in the path of progress for the State, but not without a cost that continues to this very day, a subject for another volume.[9]

---

[9] The author worked in this aviation segment for over a decade

With helicopters in the territory a downed plane and passengers were not without hope; this if word could get out asking for assistance, and by using the fuel *stash* concept to extend their normally short range. When more powerful machines came into play, where no stash or refueling point was available, the ship would "sling load" its own extra fuel in barrels and land at will to refuel on the trip out and back in order to extend its normally limited range.

Word of a mishap would typically come by radio, relay or even walk-in; the luckless pilot appearing disheveled, dirty and dejected, relating his tale of woe, where and why. If the damage was too extensive for repair on the spot, the broken craft could also be brought out in a "sling load," this sometimes in pieces, cabled to the belly of the ship and flown to the nearest point where civilization touched, there to be loaded out by truck, cat or barge, then to be repaired and fly another day.

Often early spring would mark the most favorable recovery season, this before the snow left when tracked vehicles could reach some halfway point in good weather; then the wreck was loaded out, but usually at great effort and expense. In a general sense this is how the heli and fixed wing crews took care of each other. Sometimes it worked the other way around for either party.

In the last years DC-3s, C-123's and finally C-130 Hercules were used in the S&R work, (as provided by Uncle Sam) the term being "put up a Herc" this in response to overdue or Mayday calling aircraft, as these ships could affect a search effort and stay on location for many hours. The "Hercs" also capable of in-flight refueling of the

Airforce search helicopters, all a pretty sight for the lost or downed knowing help was on the way, the search teams often working on conjunction with local spotter aircraft.

In winter the wheels came off and skis went on, the country becoming a massive white landing zone, especially the lakes, of which there were thousands. At least you could land safe once for pretty sure, uncertain of departure however. That's when the wolfing was done, a profitable but deadly game, there being no margin for error. To accomplish this one must fly low, watching the animal and ground with a quick roving eye, but sometimes in the excitement of the moment they would shoot off a strut and down they came.

Putting up a "Herc"

Some planes performed one-way landings attempting to recover a wolf, which on set-down would knock away a strut or catch a wing tip in the snow. It was easy to crash in the white on white sky and ground, as depth perception was tricky, which was called a "white-out."

For example, one heli crew found themselves trapped in such a deceptive "white out" unable to safely land. Flying along straight and level and trying to find the ground, they happily sighted a 55 gallon fuel barrel for a landing reference, only to crash instantly...they finding the mistaken object actually a pop can! Though lucky to be alive and uninjured, their ship was a total loss, they getting a bonus of a free night's sleep on the company in the broken cabin. Crashing and becoming injured in minus 50 degree temperatures was a grueling experience. All you could do was get into the meager survival canister, (we used plastic buckets crammed with food and sleeping bags, some equipped with a liner to stop blood from ruining the insulation) unrack the required travel firearm and hold out the best you could, waiting for the rescuers to show. I knew of wolfers' which held out for a week or more like this waiting to be found.

Others pursued the White Bears on the ice for big guiding cash, but the drifting pack could move a hundred miles or more in an overnight storm on you, so in and out same day was the rule. One such incident caused two new aircraft to be "misplaced" once, as they were unable to start in the cold, [10] this after landing to chase a Big White one. The story goes they were luckily happened upon by another

_____

[10] The aircraft were the new Maule M-Four-220, equipped with a Franklin engine untested in cold temperatures

scouting aircraft, this able pilot extracting all souls with a death defying takeoff is his Cub, being massively overloaded with a party of five souls aboard! Unhappily upon return to recover their new winged investments, the ice-pack had moved and their expensive craft were never to be seen again. Such were the risks flying in the Arctic, a daily gamble in the air.

Then there was the Russian problem and the cocky Mig pilots, which could end badly. The Alaska Supplement FAA handbook issued to us had a section covering such encounters, suggesting that if jumped by Migs, simply fly straight and level with your landing lights on and maybe the 20MM cannon rounds wouldn't be flying through your fabric quite so quickly. The Ruskies added a polite comment for us mentioning that if you didn't comply with this directive; "your safety was not guaranteed." We often wondered what happened to some of the bear guides that never came home, if the Russians had kept their side of the bargain or decided to make target drones out of our folks. We knew every Ruskie hotshot pilot was accountable for every round fired, so if they did pull that red colored trigger on the handgrip they were under orders to do so or were courts marshaled. It was only a game of cat and mouse 99% of the time, such antics ending when the radar sites were installed that could alert our F-Four crews to deal with them scrambling from the outposts.[11]

---

[11] The ADIZ interlocking radar system

4

Mt McKinley

The Wild Country

The old trappers and natives told stories about the massive caribou herds, their numbers carpeting the land making trails that were rutted deep into the tundra from a thousand years of movement, like the great buffalo herds of the Old West. One could relive this out there, and so who could miss that? There were moose too, places where you could see their huge racks rocking back and forth above the willows along rivers that ran far into the white winter haze, contrasting like black spots on a white canvas. White doll rams were said to be like so many flocks of sheep carpeting the hills, stalked by packs of the "one's who ran in packs," they trotting along in single file hunting strings, their black and grey hides worth the price of a drum of 80/87 fuel; a dozen a new overhaul on your engine or even down payment on a new ship if you could find a bank to help. Then there are the Brown ones, seen digging roots up in the high valleys or stalking close when you put down an animal or crashed. (Each of the above would often come straight to a crash site.) Gold was there also; ready to be panned in some uncharted creek or valley known only to the rock chuck or ptarmigan. This is how it had been for a thousand years; it was in this place the story takes place, and then it was over; the government came and the *Long Hunters* were forced out, leaving the caribou, sheep, bear, wolf and moose roaming, seen now by the brown-shirts and the well healed from down south, they who know it all from their books. That was the year Hutcheson didn't come in, best wolfer in the country they said, *Last of the Long Hunters.* We never saw him or his Champ again, he was last seen in the Brooks. God rest his soul.

5

The Beginnings of Men

It was a crisp April morning at the trailhead. Looking northeast, you could see the dark Matterhorn spires of the high country contrasting a bright blue sky. Between them was a mile of blue glacial ice. Beyond was the mother lode of the ice cap itself, and then the border country. This one was 800 miles long and 100 wide. The range itself was endless; 1500 miles plus in length. It stretched from down south all the way up to the Dezadeash country north of us and on to the McKenzie itself, a place where the aviation maps were still empty. The river was glacier blue-grey silt-water, it slipping by in silence…the whole place was silence, interrupted by the calls of the ravens, they sending out their warning calls that men were on the trail heading in. A big glacier lake was ahead of us, it sat in silence at the foot of the spires. There was willow then some ponds and a remote and unnamed tributary at the head of it all. We were heading there.

Two heavy packs lay on the snow loaded with our camp, food and traps. One large caliber rifle lay across a green "Hillary" backpack. That was mine. You never shot beaver, the weapon was for protection. We oriented a "drowning set" that at the moment the beaver was caught he dove for deep water. There was a shallow and deep stake placed with a wire between them and a one-way "dog" attached to the trap. When he tripped the pan he dove, the dog device moving deeper with him. This kept him down and from getting another breath. It saved the pelt. I sometimes thought about this, but I also thought about the dead ones we saw on the beaches. When beaver overpopulate they fight and the losers are pushed out of a valley by their own kin. The refugees are forced to take to the saltwater that kills most of them. The idea is that we take that remainder.

More than the river crossings on rotten ice, cold, weather changes, (it can snow 5 feet overnight, trapping you in) hypothermia, slides or slipping off a cliff, there was the Bruno problem. This was their county, their territory and *they* knew it. It was like there was an unposted sign at the jump-off point—"enter at your own risk—killers dwell here." And kill they did. We both knew the risk, it was an unsaid thing. I picked up the weapon and loaded it, left one out of the chamber. My dad had taught me well, drilled it into me. They called him Daniel Boone in the National Guard. He was such a good shot they kept him out of the war and had him train new recruits and travel to base shooting contests. The commander did that to him. His buddies had to fight a terrible war without him. They knew he would have helped save a few and so did he. Some never came home and of the number that did some never forgave dad for not being there. My dad never forgave that base commander, though he likely saved his life and now I'm here.

We loaded up and started in. There was a full day's work ahead. The packs are heavy and there's not even fur in them yet. If there was a lot of snow on the trail we switched lead, but today is good. I had a special glove on my rifle carrying hand; it had a flap so I could get my fingers out quickly. You had to stop and make checks. Once in a while you could get a glimpse of the upper country that filtered through the tall spruce: its beauty was staggering, even if you had been doing this a long time, you never got used to it. We felt good and joked along on the trail, eyes open and scanning though, the ravens were giving away our position. Don't know why we let those black coated spies get on like this. To be honest, they would actually turncoat and help us once in a while. Here's how it worked: if you put an animal like a moose down most often you couldn't get all the meat out in a day. That's when Bruno would move in and claim the kill as his. When you came back and Bruno was there, he would hide and just freeze to see if you were just passing or coming in and take "his" meat. He would then wait until he had maximum advantage and then either perform a warning charge, or worse, a kill charge. An old guide had taught me a trick— he said, "Kid, if the birds are in the trees, the bear is on the kill" simple as that. He was right. That was how the ravens and magpies helped us so we put up with them.

We worked slowly along the trail, level at first, crawling over a tree fall here, negotiating a cliff there. One place the trail went right over the top of a beaver hut. If you could see ahead you would stop and watch for movement. There was one spot on the trail where we were very careful. This is where Bruno struck and won once. There was a trail crew in here and one guy had straggled. It was a few years back but we weren't going to let him get away with that again. Mick's dad told us about it. Mick's dad was smart. We stopped to take a break. You had to be careful at breaks; if Bruno saw you he could try to sneak up on your backside or position himself for an ambush ahead. This was springtime; when the boars emerged from their dens and they were careless, love struck and hungry—the most dangerous time of the year. Same if you parked your boat on the bank or crashed an airplane. You NEVER separated. They feared two, but one alone was vulnerable. That was rule #1 in bear country, stay together.

We warmed from the work. First off were the heavy wool jackets, then wool hat and finally the gloves. If the temp came up to 20 or 30, which it would in April from the sun reflecting off the snow, we would even be in tee-shirts. We always chatted. This let Bruno know we were approaching and to beware. We were high schooler's: so we talked about all that high schooler's talk about - girls, class, the teachers, country and the game. We talked excitedly about the potential of this new territory for a successful take. The tributary we were headed for was located last year coming out. It looked full of beaver and other fur. We had seen other sign too. We understood Bruno but not the girls. We were an outside group anyway. Most of the girls liked cars and jocks. We talked about the jocks good and bad. We learned that for the most part, one night in bear country and a jock became a chicken. As for the girls, they could care less about what we did out here, but we had a bond they would never understand. After 4 hours of hard hiking we were nearing camp and the girl subject got shelved. Time to set camp and cross the river.

The Great Arctic River

Pat

Rivers are wonderful things but they have two sides: one, they are pretty to look at; two: they are hard to cross without a boat. There's no way to get a boat up into this country. There is one logjam after another on this river and if anyone could get a jetboat here, the whole area could be hunted out. That's what makes it good for us. We are willing to pack in and stay in bear country, most are not. The camp is now up and we begin our search for a crossing point. The river is free of ice but swift. This is where my buddy Pat comes in, he's as sure-footed as a mule. If anyone can pick a way across, it's him. We load up our day packs and strike out.

We use hip-boots here. You fly in them, hike in them and sometimes sleep in them. Hip-boots are a trapper's footwear. First thing is, you get the best there is, second; you keep them dry. Hip-boots are the hardest boot in the world to dry if you dowse them. That's rule #2: NEVER go over your hip-boots. You can't build a fire in this part of the country to dry them without a chainsaw and gallons of gas. One time I packed in a gallon mixed with oil bound and determined to make a fire. All I did was watch it go up in black smoke—and still no fire. Even a local wolverine thought it was entertaining watching me try...

Pat expertly picks his way across the 80 yard stretch of swift water and miraculously it was pretty shallow all the way over. That was a super good break; we had found a superb crossing. You could have never guessed it looking over from the other bank, we had hit the jackpot. No other trapper would have found this in a million years. We were in pristine trapping territory now!

Pat carefully works his way across keeping me informed as he puts his foot on the other bank, looking out for Bruno.

Bruno can't be trusted. They will watch you get all the way across and then bolt. Good for us, once they see there are two of us, they feel outnumbered. If one was there watching us, he knew there was some open ground to cover in order to get at Pat ... but then he'd be exposed several seconds before he could spring on him. In that amount of time he would have caught one or two 220 grain rounds of silver-tip 308 Winchester along his neck, that impact downing him for a moment. While he was twirling I would have punched in the last four core-lock rounds[12] while Pat retreated back across the river. Instead, it all ended fine. No Bruno. I have the gun and Pat was the one who was exposed. "We're going to have to watch ourselves in here," I comment. We find tracks. "One was in here eating last year's huckleberries" Pat reports. "So they're up already," I come back.

Early up Browns are usually digging roots in the alpine country this time of year, but not this boy. I work my way around the willow covered island and see where our friend had walked out. His track was there, all 12" of it. "Look at this," I said pointing at the clear print on the bank. "This boy is a 10 to 12 footer. I think I've played cat and mouse with this guy before; one time mid-winter we trailed him following another hunter heading inland, he figured out he was sandwiched and cut out. He's old and wise. Likely knows what a gun can do too. He doesn't hate man or my gun would be smoking and you would be one wet Patrick, but it would have been fun watching you crossing the Eagle with Bruno on your tail!" "Shuuut uuup," Pat spats back half-heartedly. "Enough whining, let's get trapping!" "You're right!" I quip back and we start up the creek.

---

[12] A round with a tip that held together and would break bone. You had to mechanically break down a big bear

Crossing

Trekking in bear country is like this: long periods of boredom interrupted by moments of sheer terror. I was thinking - wow, only in Alaska. We had worked the situation like pros, though Pat was the oldest at 17. In bear country it's like you're are on a sapper mission in enemy territory; you go in, steal Bruno's stuff and get out. If you keep in mind where you are and what you're up against you can stay out of those teeth and claws; both of us had seen what they could do to a man. There were a few men walking around our town with limps and one with a disfigured face. That's why I practiced about every other week or so; 20 rounds at a time with ball ammo. My shoulder was always a little black and blue. That's why I carried the gun.

Anticipation was high now. We were in virgin Alaskan territory as wild as any man has seen. We worked our way deeper into the wilderness and set all the gear we had. To keep safe in this process, I would get on a high spot and ride shotgun, round chambered and thumb on the safety, while Pat would wade into the freezing slough water setting the deep-poles. I knew Bruno was out there; and I yelled a challenge out a few times like, "come on out and meet your maker" (my favorite bear challenge after John Wayne in the movie "True Grit") or just talk loud to Pat while he was in the water. It wasn't the last time I would have to use that phase and really mean it: a story for another time. We saw no more of the big guy and we were safely across the river by dark. There were fewer Bruno on that side.

Nights in Bear Country

The most important thing to remember about camp placement in bear country is to stay off the main trail. Second is don't leave food around – dirty dishes, pots and pans and the like. Mark the trail yourself on the walkin route to your camp. Then Bruno knows what he's dealing with. If you're invading his protected territory look out. If you know the country this will be obvious. Don't camp near salmon spawning areas or berry patches. Make it hard for him to creep up on you. Bears don't like to cross open areas or water to approach a man-camp. In our case we were on a peninsula with water on three sides and a river. We faced our tent opening to the approach side and sometimes added brush so he had to make noise to get close. They hate that. Think of the general wind direction. They can smell your food ¼ mile away and come right in like a hungry dog. Never have any kind blood in camp

EVER. Cut your game far away. I'm very serious about this. Lastly, always sleep with your rifles loaded.

Bears have two types of charges – the first is an intimidation charge. He will test your nerve in this. We shoot high in this phase to scare him. He may turn around and do it again just as fast. This time he may come closer. Move away each time. Third time shoot him down right when he wheels around to go at it again. This way you will get a clean side shot. A bear was once found with a full load of buckshot right between the eyes grown over. What happened to the hunter was never known. Understand they are near impossible to stop when in the adrenaline rush. They can run 100 yards flat out with no heart. I would shoot them in a shoulder first if they were angry. They are slower on three legs.

The kill charge is something different altogether. This is a full speed no-holds-barred attack. He will not let up. In this phase he's determined that he has the advantage, and no matter how fast you run, even faster than a deer, he wants to catch you and kill you for food. I don't know anyone who has survived a surprise kill charge without getting mauled, even with guns blazing. In all cases of kill charge attacks I know of, the bear did not see the man's partner. I will say this type of attack is the one where most people are killed if by themselves and unarmed. Many fully armed people are killed this way. Any more detail would not be appropriate here. I was kill charged once. This by a wounded bear but I knew where he was. He died rolling past me on a steep hill. He was so close I could see the whites of his eyes, teeth and claws. I didn't even quiver. If I had not known his location it could have ended a lot worse.

That night was great. We watched the beaver in a pond near camp and learned a lot about their nocturnal activity in the moon light. They acted as free as birds frolicking in the spring breakup warmth after a hard winter. We hit the sack tired and happy, knowing if Bruno was around we would hear a slap on the water from the beaver alarming his approach. Next morning was still and overcast. We anxiously got up, dressed and crossed the river. Every set was full but one. We skinned our catch and put one carcass high in a tree. Next day it was gone, the tell tale claw marks two inches spaced and 12 feet high. It was one of our big friends. There was not a track to be found. We had learned to get along.

Specks on the Mountain

Mick

The dory was pounding into the jaws of the great inlet and the water was changing color from blue to brownish grey. Mountains towered on both sides of us and the sky was thin overcast. We had seven tanks of six gallons each aboard and the third was on the fuel line. That's what determined your range, the fuel in those tanks. There were three major glaciers that fed the inlet and a major river plowing into the sea right here. The flank of the mountain on the right came down from 6,000 feet dead into the water before us, trying to block the river. Make it around that reef and the whirlpool full of seal below it and you were into the river itself. This one ran hundreds of miles northeast all the way into Canada. We were heading to the border country. The closer we got the calmer the water and the smiles came out. The saltwater run was about over and we were in beautiful country miles from nothing. Up ahead the next challenge lay before us—the sandbars. All Alaska river's have sandbars where they enter the sea. Sandbars are a pain. Before you go you always check the tide books. You fix one time for high tide in your head and then use math on your feet the rest of the trip. Six hours to low, plus 45 minutes, plus six more to high. We were late. The current was rushing out of the inlet in torrents.

At this point you need to learn to read the river. You had to tack in fast on step going flat out. It was all or nothing to cross it or spend 10 hours on the bar or worse: push for hours hoping to find enough water to chug along, and that was rare. The objective of the trip was out ahead 15 miles up valley. The peak loomed high looking down at us. Past it was the Alaska/Canada border. On it were white specks. They were out today. Those were mountain goats. We wanted one of those. To get one you had to climb. Not only that, you had to go through the devil's club zone for 1,000 feet then negotiate the cliffs. Devils club was a perfect name for a spring-loaded stick full of nettles that's pointed downhill; springing back when brushed. That's why those specks were safe and happy up there. Only stupid boys went after them. This was my second trip so I guess that makes me twice as stupid. The climb to them was 5,300 feet, one way. You had to hike in a mile, climb for them and get out in the same day. Last time I was there we nearly died. I missed my shot and my partner downed him. It was the last big game animal I ever missed in Alaska. The weather came in and we dropped into the wrong canyon coming out. A steep blind canyon—this with a big goat in our packs and our legs jello. It started raining and snowing and we were soaked to the skin. You can't get your traction in those conditions. But we made it out and were back the year following.

This was the life we lived and places we traveled in those times. Running the wild saltwater inland sea to get to the mouths of even wilder rivers. Hiking into the glacial valleys and not a soul near for 50, 100 miles or more, some unvisited since the gold rush a century before. We would see the marks of the old camps—tin cans, bottles and the like. They had come, searched for color and left. The whole country was left to us it seemed, we the only ones that cared in the world. We hunted, trapped, fished, piloted vessels or fast flat-bottomed dories, all when we were teenagers; some of us even flew airplanes. We shot moose, mountain goats and sheep, deer, bear and caribou. We sold our fur, saved our pennies and filled our lives with the country. We dreamed up trips no one thought could be done and did them. We dodged the bears and elements like the best of them and won—most of the time.

The First Hint there was Someone Watching Us

We thought little about church or God. It wasn't mentioned save in vain. One time when we were in the upper country I chased a band of goats into a ravine and shot one off a cliff. This was stupid because I likely couldn't have got it out, but when you're 16 and have an easy chance at these boys you pull the trigger and sort things out later. We typically carried a hundred foot of parachute cord wrapped around our waist while hunting them, this in case you got caught in a tough spot and used

39

to let yourself down. Because we were trapping I didn't have mine with me. This would be my undoing ... almost.

I worked my way around the lateral moraine high on the left side of the glacier cut. I was up a few hundred feet from the ice itself, the scrapped flat granite walls stretching high above and below me. It was raining and cold. I figured the animal had fallen at about this spot. It was a long shot and I saw him fall about here. There was a 6" ledge going in the direction I needed to head, and Pat was above watching. He knew it was chancy. He being about twice as goat-footed as me, his cautions should have been a warning, but nerve builds on nerve when you have an audience and I was going to do all I could to retrieve that animal. We had a code about this sort of thing and wounded bears, the latter a story for another time.

It was at this point I realized I had gone a bridge too far. I started to retreat and that option wasn't going well. I yelled to Pat that I was in trouble. He got as close as he could above me but was still too far with no rope. Then of all the things to happen: it started to rain hard and not only rain, but *ice rain*. I unlimbered my rifle strap and threw it up as high as I could, but still it fell many feet short. At that point I felt myself slipping. This is not your average slip on a sidewalk; this is a 300 foot fall into the abyss. While attempting to throw the sling up for the last time I felt myself go. At that moment I saw my whole life pass before me like a movie—as a baby on the couch with our first dog, other scenes from when I was growing up...and then I woke up; not splattered among the riding boulders below but on a safe ledge above! I looked around and brushed off the gravel that had imbedded in my damp jeans. I peered up to see the bewilderment on Pat's face, who just as quick blurted out, "How'd you to that?"

"I dunno," I say back, and he says, "Let's get out of here!" We did and that was that. The incident was never talked about again. When he did, people would look over at me puzzled; but it never got me favor with a girl or anything.

My next spiritual experience (if you want to call it that) was as a senior listening to the radio driving into school one November morning. That time of year is terribly dangerous to fly or float in Southeast Alaska. The storms can be horrific and temperatures can drop two dozen degrees in a few minutes. Winds could stir from 10 to 90Mph instantly and wreak havoc at sea and air before anything could be done about it. In those conditions nothing can save you when storms like those struck at the wrong time. I used to think that to live or die was just a toss of the coin—fate and luck the sole determinates you know.

Back at school I had a hero. If there was a life to be lived it would have been Rick's. He had access to much more territory and more; Rick had been flying his own aircraft since he was 16. He and his buddy got out and trapped some amazing country with that thing, while Pat, Mick and I didn't even have a car. We hitchhiked or took my dory (later Mick did have wheels). A lot of territory could be had by a boat; but we secretly coveted the airplane.

Rick had gone on to be a well-known bush pilot. I didn't know him well but followed his stories. We were living out our own adventures by then. That morning the radio announced that a tragic flying accident had occurred and Rick was gone. Worse, he had a young family and baby aboard and all had perished. That news went deep in me. We had an airliner crash the day before school a few years before; all aboard were lost in the same kind of storm. I was on the jet behind them; our radio-compass got us through the mountains, theirs got distorted. Next day, a Monday, the seats in class were salt and pepper occupied; the teacher foolishly calling out the roster…the kids present reminding the guy why they were absent. I thought, "Wow, obviously this guy is new." Some of the girls broke down. On this latest news I decided in my heart that there was no God.

6

The M-Four

Long Hunters

A light breeze was blowing down the big river. All across the plain stretching out to the Brooks the rust colored brush weaved along, contrasted by fingers of green spruce and taiga that made a beautiful quilt-work across the valley. Beyond the plain the grey peaks of the Brooks loomed upward, pushing higher and higher in an endless maze stretching off past the horizon. A dusting of snow swept their north flanks, and yellow leaves of the willows floated down close to me with a rustling sound in the

43

breeze, piling among the white roots and grey rocks sticking out here and there along the river bank. That was the only sound that broke the silence, the silence of the Arctic. It is heard and understood only by those who experience it. The sweet smell of the softwoods was in the air, just as it had been for 20 centuries of falls gone by. It was a painting with a crystal river running through—this was fall in the Arctic and there was nothing like it in the world.

The machine sat silent on the gravel bar of this Great Arctic River, her wings tied down to logs under rock piles to keep her from flipping over in a gust. A breeze of 40 will lift a 1000 pounds per wing you see, and more than one pilot returned to find his ship wrong side up while away. But that's the way it is here, there being no room for error, that is, error between man and machine against the elements, the elements ever winning and teaching another lesson.

This bar was about 50 by 400 feet with a good approach north and south bleeding into the river, the ship having big tires for the rocks and soft spots for this type of work. There's a line of mud dobs under both wings above the tires, this caused on touch-down by the tires slinging up the river muck pelting the underside of the aluminum wings with a sharp *"RATATAT...TAT"* report. This alarmed new passengers, but they would get used to it, there would be more lessons before we got out of the country this fall. We were two hours out from the last stash, distance here figured in hours of flight-time fuel. The hunters are excited and getting ready; we are almost set to go looking for the 'bou!

The Stash

In order to stay out, recon and move independently in the country a fuel *stash* had to be brought out before the hunt. Fuel was carried in five gallon shiny square tins of 80/87 avgas, every drop needed to feed the thirsty Continental, Pratt & Whitney or Lycoming engines used in these aircraft. Bought new, they came in a wooden case of two tins that weighed full about sixty-five pounds. Most of us had odd assortment of used tins, those picked up here and there then refilled in town. The high paid guides from Anchorage had new cases and left the empties around, so one way or another you collected your own set of them. Once the fuel stash was set we ranged freely into the depths of the *Arctic*, the frontier free before us for the taking.

To put out a stash, you topped off in town or selected jump-off point (town being the last point north with fuel and a road) cramming in all the fuel you could get in the wing tanks and twisting the gas caps on tight. If they weren't snug or the seals bad, your engine's life blood could secretly siphon off in an unseen vapor trail behind you, potentially bringing the flight to an end at the wrong place. Seats and unneeded gear were stripped out to save weight and space for tins (even the battery was not exempt, especially in the Three Eighteens). Stuffed to the ceiling with full tins on all sides, a takeoff loaded like this could be dicey; you had to get off and gain enough altitude to clear any forward obstacles, then wait for fuel burn in trade for weight and distance, throttle wide open, a minute of flight time making 80mph being one and a half *miles*.

Any miscalculation and you couldn't climb but a few feet and were doomed, as more than one pilot lost life or limb staggering off heavy like this. Of course the FAA looked down on this sort of thing ... you had to plan right because there was no banking away from obstacles loaded like this. Banking just a tad could cause the wing on the inside to stall, then on your back you would go, upside down and *in* as quick as a flash. Many, many fine pilots perished this way, some with a full load of passengers, but not me in this ship. I had learned from them and that's all I'll say about that.

Fill times and quantity were penned on the palm of your hand, chart or on a kneepad. You copied your hour meter numbers and wrote the word "Full" next to them like "2356.6 hrs Full." The number part measured total time that ship had flown, this in a little window that is part of the instrument, "Full" the most important four letter word in the Bush.

Once at cruise altitude the M-Four made 120mph or 2 miles per minute. Today she was loaded with 65 gallons in 13 tins inside plus 42 in the wings. Heavy, she needed nine+ gallons/hour to feed the Continental so the plan was to fly 3-4 hours out then look for a place to land near the game. This size stash could get us across the Brooks and even to the Arctic coast with fuel to spare. Or that was the plan anyway.

It was a smooth clear morning for the trip, so I got in and organized the cockpit, putting everything I needed in reach for the four hour run: maps, pen, water, food, Alaska Supplement guide and etc., rifle and survival gear stuffed in too. After a good look at the ship I jumped in, looked around and said "OK, good" as a habit. Then I ran through my checklist: Ropes off, fuel caps and oil cover on, tanks both, mixture rich and the rest. I primed the engine with the big silver hand primer in the panel center—three pumps then in, turn and lock. Before start I looked around and called out "CLEAR." Closing the master and turning the start switch she comes to life—Bruuum Ba Bruum Buum Buum... the silence now over for hours, the cabin shaking with the big idling 6. When cold they shake more, this because of valve clearance vs. cold cylinder length. A light mixture of avgas, leather and oil aroma swirl in the cockpit now, the sleeping ship alive and dew inside the windshield drying from the vents. By habit my door is cracked, the prop slipstream blowing air around the cabin. First scan was oil pressure, and after idling a minute or two a full gage scan commences, the first of a hundred on a long run like this. Then it was OK to go to high idle, like 1200, and check the mags early, why run for 10 minutes and find something amiss now? Then back to idle once some cylinder and oil temps came up. I move all the flight controls and make a radio call. Another gage scan including fuel and we're rolling toward runway 36—that's short for 360—*north*.

While rolling another magneto check is in order. I add in some throttle and 2000 rpm shows on the tach, the cockpit alive now as I select mag Left..., wait... Right, wait..., now both, and good. This step checks all 12 spark plugs in the dual ignition system, 2 per cylinder. Now carburetor heat on, wait ... wait ... and back in, making sure no ice is built up. You always need to be patient with these check's, some pilots get too antsy at this stage to their foolish peril. An air-cooled engine can quickly build ice in the throat of the carburetor and absolutely must be checked before a takeoff. Flaps 15, the lever comes up and clicks next to my seat. Time to think again now, double check it all; gages, breakers, the list is repeated I saying to myself, "Don't miss a checklist item, get ahead of this ship all the way out and back today." Satisfied, a peaceful calm settles over me, the training and experience committees meet in my mind and say, "you're ready to go." Always listen to your conscience and don't skip items is the rule. Better a little embarrassment now and a taxi back to the ramp than be chastised later. The rpm is put to 1000 and I roll out looking down this big paved runway, about to launch this load northbound.

Cleared by the tower guy I roll into position and hesitate a bit to set the DG, looking at the compass to see if they align with the runway numbers. Double check the wind, the wind … I glance left and view the orange wind sock, - light and down the runway it shows me, OK, but the tower could give you the wrong runway, so you have to double check yourself. As PIC you have absolute authority to reject his runway choice for you, that's the rule, you are 'Pilot in Command' and responsible for the safety of the flight and passengers. He knows that up there but likes to think you're his ward. You can be nice at first, but if they get snotty then be assertive; always remembering sometimes it can work the other way around, like he catches *you* fouling up…and that's good, so think team.

He also may try to act like he's God but he's not, don't let him order you around if you know you're right. I'll be glad to get free of this airspace. Where I'm heading there's no one to boss me around. That's the last item on the checklist, drilled into my head a thousand times. So many pilots have a lax attitude about that little piece of paper and missed one stupid thing to their demise, but not me, I use the thing, it's stupid not to. I scan the airspace and open the throttle to full power, the cockpit loud and shaking now as she moves briskly down the runway being pulled by the big 6 and the scanning starts, airspeed-runway, airspeed-runway ... airspeed ... 60 ... 70 ... Ok, NOW!—I rotate and she comes off nice, naturally feeling heavy with all this fuel onboard, it's expected I think to myself. The VSI is telling the story now; 300 vertical feet per minute, the airspeed needle reads 80 mph, perfect. I hold the heading for the "straight out" departure and drop the notch out of the flaps and cleanup, scanning the airspace around me for traffic and the gage groups; oil, rpm, airspeed, the purring of the 6 filling the cabin. I can relax now, all is fine. Glancing back, the footprint of the runway layout is growing smaller behind me, and five miles out I'm finally free of the government and tower Gods. One more important radio call to make, file a flight plan with Flight Service. It's amazing the search forces that can be activated by that simple little call, and how abandoned a pilot feels if he fails to do so and later gets himself into a jam. In Alaska, a flight plan can be made for weeks allowing for the hunters, prospectors etc. to get out there do their business and get back, or at least check back. If you're late, they put a Herc up for you, a Herc being a big 4 engine military job with big gas tanks, also called a C-130, capable of extended time over the search zone, you being a needle in a haystack, or more like a 1000 acre hayfield in this country. We all liked the 130s. Before that they used C-123s. Twice they were called out for me, a subject for another time.

Out past civilization and airborne, the numberless tundra hills stretch out before me, each slipping beneath me one by one like a silent movie. It's just you, your ship and number one engine in this theater of wilderness, without evidence of man in any direction. We always joked about calling the engine "*number one,*" cuz we never had a number two. If number one failed you could disappear for good, especially if no one heard your Mayday call, which most often gave you lonely static on the headset in the answerback. I wore a WWII military job, it was made from parts of a few company throwaways.

Calculating 2 miles-a-minute flying at 120 Mph meant 20 minutes after takeoff your radio would not reach civilization. If you came up on the emergency channel, a heavy could pick you up, like the FBX-Kaktovic run ship, but that window was only about 15 minutes long once a week on Fridays, he tacking up and back to the Chuckchi Sea. If you were down you always remembered the time he overflew, then would try some calls. That crew was good and kept on the lookout for that kind of thing. They were mostly Long Hunters themselves doing their day job like me. I even relayed with a Canadian Airforce Herc at the Pole once, and met the nice fellow years later, he then a 747 captain on a trip to Joburg.

An hour out now, the fuel gage needles start to wag off of the "Full" mark, running on one tank an hour, then switch to the other and back kept the wings balanced. The fuel selector valve by my left knee has three positions,

"Left", "Both" and "Right," left or right for each wing tank and separate gages for each on the instrument panel. Fuel gages good mostly for two things; telling you if you have a leak and if the tanks are full or empty. One time on a 900 mile run I noticed the gages dropping fast; upon making an emergency landing in Canada I jumped out and was struck by the smell of avgas running all down the side of the ship, including around the white-hot exhaust pipes. Another mechanic had cross threaded the fuel bowl. Down south mechanics can't be trusted, or so I thought. So you flew on time, that was how we did it here, never trust the gages ... *gallons consumed an hour* and those numbers written on your hand. I had no idea how important those numbers and needles would become in the coming weeks.

The airspeed indicator sat near the gages also; the number one use for it was to set your *landing speed.* If you were short of the touchdown spot and it said less than 40 you crashed ... simple as that. On the landing phase you had to scan fast—airspeed, ground-airspeed-ground out the corner of your eye when landing on these postage stamps out here. Once I was doing a flyby of a big strip by my standards; the agitated passenger asking "where are we going to land?" He expecting a paved strip or something out of a movie I guess. Then I swung around right over the top of the racks of the caribou bulls standing there and set down upslope. He was a little white knuckled to say the least, but this stuff was normal for us. Shorter then even Mel Gibson's play-games in "Air America" every day.

The rest of the stash flight you could relax and enjoy the country, watching the compass heading, DG, altitude and do some map reading. A "DG" or Directional

Gyro was nice. It gave you a solid emulation of your magnetic compass heading but was more precise; and didn't bounce around. It would need correcting every 20 minutes. To correct, you needed fairly smooth air and pushed in a little knob and set it to match the compass, simple as that. You better watch your map too: one missed river fork or wrong canyon could cost you hours of back tracking, this error resulting in more than one crisis for some outstanding pilots. I spent a lot of time on the map when flying the Three Eighteens, especially when on the deck in weather, which was much of the time in winter. After fuel exhaustion, weather was the real killer out here. Forecasting was just that, an educated guess by guys 500+ miles and several mountain ranges away. They had no satellite view and few ground reporting stations in those days. If we did get in contact they relished our pilot reports then passed them out.

Sometimes you had two or three mountain passes to traverse on a stash run, so if you flew beyond the point of no return (which we often did) and got trapped, your fuel remaining was possibly insufficient to get back to a landing spot. If the weather closed in behind you this could be really bad news, trapping you between the ranges with no *out*. Having an *out* was always part of planning; no one else could help you out here once airborne. Sad part was, when we searched for those unlucky guys the weather would be better, so you could never piece together the real story, as rarely could a guy get a call off for anyone to hear it, the distances simply being too great and few had HF long range sets. Your end could be a sad and lonely one with nobody but the Almighty in witness, leaving those left behind with little more but a pile of sheet metal and memories for closure. Such tragedy repeats every year in Alaska. Newcomer beware.

There were few radio outlets connected to the FAA in those days, called RCOs, these would work if you were close or high enough for the signal to reach them. We would stay on that channel to keep track of things and other pilots around us, (which was rare) the FAA fight service guys right on top of those for us, they often pilots themselves. We knew exactly when we were in range of those babies, often doglegging or climbing to include them in our route. These channels we stayed up on: sometimes to hear the helplessness in a pilot's voice that was in trouble. This really got to you sometimes, we being helpless to help them. As they were not relays, often we could only hear a conversation one-way, our radio not having the power to reach either party. Then there was the sound of the Emergency Location Transmitter or *ELT*. We all carried one aboard with its chilling howl when activated, designed to go off on impact—*forward* impact. To help in a search, you tuned the comm. radio to 121.5 MHz and flew a pattern: away the sound got weaker, toward stronger. It was a sickening eerie sound. We all hated it but had to stay tuned to find them. Enough of that for now.

Stash runs were best characterized as "long periods of boredom interrupted by moments of sheer terror," the latter being the landing part. Slinging a thousand pounds of fuel at 100 feet-per-second could be a little unnerving you see, especially at postage stamp runways with white-hot exhaust stacks. That was the real deal.

53

The cockpit smelled of the 80/87 from the tins, and whistle of fresh air was coming in from the vents. You scanned the gages and listened in on the ADF radio (automatic direction finder) for entertainment, that is if you were lucky enough to afford one. The ADF has a needle that always points to the station selected (if in range) and no matter how lost you were the ADF never was. Out here it was always tuned to one of the big 100,000 watt AM stations like Nome, Fairbanks or maybe Glenallen. Funny that Glennallen always came in better than Fairbanks, it being 400 miles and a mountain range further from the former. Each day a program would come on, like "Caribou Clatter," or "Village Hotline," these transmitting music, news, weather and a general message board for the villages and out-stations at specified times. When you lost them that was when you really felt disconnected from it all. I had a WWII headset over my navy blue wool cap to listen in, same that we used in the Three Eighteens, as they were terribly loud. A few folks had their own HF (high frequency) ground sets to call civilization from the bush, but most everyone gathered around their AM sets and listened in to these programs in the villages, as a message system had been set up for the benefit of these folks, a party line kindda deal and no one wanted to miss out on what was going on. The idea was that you sent a letter or called the home station on the landline, then gave them a message to be broadcast over the air. The messages could be about family, friends, etc., who was going here or there or a health report; greetings from families in other villages, birthday wishes and so forth non-stop.

It would go something like this; "Hi Charlotte K., this is Frank, Dad is fine and we expect to be on the Wien flight Tuesday if the weather is OK, see ya then, love, Frank." If someone was late coming in or lost, like a dog team, snowmobile, plane, boat etc., things would get more serious, providing updated info on the search effort and names of those in the parties, often calling for prayer for all involved etc. (I was on there for that once, a "searchee"). These three were the only stations covering a 300,000 square mile area and were very important.

My ADF training was given to me by an ex B-17 Captain that knew his stuff on that box, worth every penny of the $1000 I paid for it. When you needed to find your way home in weather or too low to read a map, it was priceless. You could even find a runway with it.

Three hours out now I could see the web of 'bou trails stretching out before me. I started the descent to the Big River, it meandering out to the north horizon, a beautiful blue ribbon of clear water and not a single sign of humanity anywhere, not even a cabin for a hundred miles. This was spectacular country to see from the air and the weather was perfect! When you took in sights like this you repeated to yourself over and over "I'm the luckiest guy on the planet," and a chill ran through you. You reflected and told yourself, "I'm Alaskan, this is it and nothing else." The trails mentioned had been made by centuries of caribou traffic and ran in deep in crisscrossed ruts. Seeing them made a guy feel real good, knowing the animals were still out there in big numbers just like a thousand years ago, not like the empty buffalo trails of the West that are gone forever. No sirree, that feeling can't be bought or sold, only

Walt taking a 180 off on water in the Brooks with a full load: "more time upside down than I had right-side up." A phase that can have two meanings

experienced. This country created emotions all Long Hunters feel, and they will sacrifice life and limb and everything else for it. The summits of the Brooks Range began looming out of the mist now. It was close to game time and this little sightseeing mission was about to end.

"Oil pressure 45, temps green, 2275 rpm steady and number one engine is running fine!" I call out loud, taking a swig of water and pushing my wool cap back. Saying this was kind of a confidence routine you know, getting the blood moving after nearly 4 hours in the seat.

The older pros were better pilots than me of course, having more flying time upside down than me right side up, they would remind me, like Pete, Anderson, Audi, Wien, Wilson and all. They needed us once in a while though: a buckled gear on the Sag, flipped on the Wind, bent prop in the Sadlerochit's or just crashed on the Copper. They had some real experiences to share though, but not for this time.

A Three Eighteen had a 526 Horse Power Turbine Engine in the back, a pilot controlled hook and a longline to sling them out. They were the finest mountain helicopter in the world and we were proud to fly them. Built in France in the '60s, they had excellent visibility in a whiteout, a great engine that ran better the more rain or snow that ran through it, lots of room and a 156 gallon fuel tank, this giving us double the range of the American ships. They would fly safely in minus 50 with modifications, and were equipped with cargo racks, high skid gear a great heater and skis—a true bush machine, for sure.

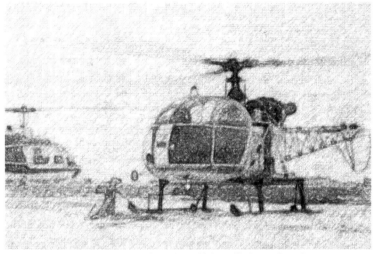

A Three Eighteen ready for take-off, headlight on in minus 40 at Deadhorse, North Slope. The ship on the left was lost in a tragic accident a few weeks later

It all started when our boss lost his best friend and chief pilot in an American built job, his engine failing when he needed it most – low, heavy with passengers and in a blizzard. It was in one of those November storms mentioned.[13] Rather than quit the business, the owner flew to France to test out a new French job called a Three Eighteen "C" with improved engine and running gear. He landed on Mt Blanc with the famous Jean Boulet[14] and when they returned said simply "put it in a box" and the rest is history. French helicopter equipment has dominated Alaska aviation ever since. I did what was needed to make them work in those temps and had some fun with them too; heck, the bosses weren't out here flying in minus 50 with no hangars. They were sitting safe and warm a 1000 miles away, sipping coffee and giving us orders, while flirting with the secretaries, we were risking our lives every day to get the job done and pay the bills. So what if we played a little, what was wrong with that? That's how I learned to fly them, bootleg time. Of course it wasn't too bad, we only checked in when we could get to a phone, which was weeks sometimes, depending where you were stationed in the bush. One big piece we did was to build mountain communication sites for projects like the Alaska Pipeline (a three year 24/7 project) or move an outlaw grizzly 100 miles from a village.

We also did rescue work when called upon. If somebody crashed we would bring in parts and/or fuel to get them airborne and see them off. If the craft had major damage, we would set up the broken plane to sling-out

---

[13] I remember hearing that report over the radio in 1969 not knowing I would be working for the same company 5 years later.

[14] Jean set the world altitude record for helicopters in a SA 315 Lama in June of 1972 at 40,814 feet. This record was exceeded by using an updraft in March 2002. The pilot admitted the same to me. Jean was a fine man and great aviation pioneer. His engine quit on the way up or he would have gone higher!

underneath us, being very important that we do this carefully, as more than one ship had been lost pulling out a busted fixed wing. The plane could start flying up on the long line you see, fouling the tail rotor or such, and then it was over, a bigger mess then when you started. It was expected to try though, so we did.

I was new kid on this block called the Arctic, but they saw my stuff and I got respect back, that was all that counted here—honor, respect and a good name. Once in a while one of the nicer guys would sit me down for coffee and tell me a few stories, then work in how to stay alive out here. These little chats saved my neck more than once I can tell you: pilots that defy the rules still die every year. Then there was the left seat time I got with my pilots, seasoned Vietnam Vets every one, most with holes in them from battle.

I will say their integrity was absolutely perfect; they having nothing to prove to anyone out there. They were a happy go lucky bunch after dodging high-speed lead for a tour or more. They told me the worst day flying the bush was still better than the best day at war. Little was said about it to me; they talked quietly about it among themselves, and that in short bursts, when they did talk about at all.

As a stupid kid I would ask how this one got some huge scar, or another what the story was about being shot through both knees landing in a hot LZ. They were real pros though, and we had a good time out there. We never compromised flying safety, though one stunt indirectly saved my life once. We would often get our nose into some real nasty weather on occasion, even for a Three Eighteen, so I got to see stuff that would kill a fixed wing pilot if you put your nose in there. This way I learned what to avoid. Once a pilot said over the intercom; "weather will kill you" in a serious tone, as we were about to crash side-slipping down some glacier trapped between layers near Valdez, trying to get back to base in one piece. I didn't answer back as he was too busy: tacking downslope to his side, I would have lived in the rollover I think.[15] The FAA doesn't teach this kind of weather safety stuff for the most part; "clear of clouds" or "one mile and clear of clouds" is all that's in the rule book. Wowsie. So "Pilot Error" was what the accident report would often read, these crashes ending so many careers and making so many widows and orphans. The fact that not one thing has been added to the actual flight training about mountain or weather flying since makes you wonder who's writing those curriculums. Even today they say more about psychology than mountain techniques in the pilot training curriculums. Military and Airline pilots have strict controls on flying, giving them radar vectors and altitudes in weather, rarely experiencing the real deal and decision making needed to fly safely here.

I should mention that the Three Eighteens always brought us home. I don't think a single pilot or passenger ever died in all the years they remained in Alaska, nor did any from the Three Fifteen Lamas that succeeded them. The Lama patrolling Mt McKinley for the Park Service from 1977-2012. Many a downed crew, lost hiker or stranded mountaineer owe their necks to them, that's for

---

[15] Bob Reeve records nearly buying it at this same location 40 years prior in the book *Glacier Pilot*

sure. I remember once the boss getting mad at a new Vet pilot that wouldn't go one day because of bad weather back at home base. An hour later we got word that one of our competitor's took the same trip had crashed with injuries. All machines have their limits. After flying with that same pilot later I really learned to respect him and the idea of setting personal flying limits. Never heard another exchange like that come down from the boss after that.

A Three Fifteen "B" Lama, "Watcher" of Mt McKinley

To give you an idea how it was, these vets would pull different pranks to distract attention from what they had just gone through in the war. For example, one of the guys had a human sized inflatable Pink Rabbit. If we got back to town for a day or two we would inflate this guy and take him out on the town with us. We would order him buttered brazed carrots for dinner and have a good laugh at the waitress's reaction. They would think we were crazy, but there was nothing wrong with what we were doing. One time the tower operator in Fairbanks was giving me a bad time over nothing, so when we left I strapped the rabbit into the copilot's seat and taped his hands to the controls. Now you have to understand a Three Eighteen has a perfectly clear cockpit bubble—you could see right through to the inside, especially on a sunny day. So we high taxied right by the tower widow then someone over the radio said "What's up Doc?" and we took off. I remember getting a call from Juneau over that, but next time the tower guy was nicer to us when we came to town.

It's a free country in the Arctic. Some didn't like newbies like me out there on the hunt, but others remembered me crewing Three Eighteens and figured I was maybe OK if we ran into each other somewhere. A few knew I had been supporting the fleet with an M-Four, but no one ever said a thing about it. Respect was everything to us, we had no room for phonies and anyway, they didn't last long out here.

Some 'bou were showing in good numbers below me. I had poked around them in minus 40 the previous winter, but today was like Hawaii, a warm, no wind day … not good with this load, as a breeze in the right direction is every pilot's friend. Dropping down I could see upriver the bars were getting smaller. I can't do a 3 with this much weight. Compass still says north, the fuel needles are bouncing on "E," and I go on.

The M-Four is no Super Cub, so you need some space to land with a load like this. They don't actually fly factory Cubs here. Here most Cubs are in name only; big propellers, extended wings, balloon tires, extra fuel tanks and large tail-planes. A good Cub could land in 2 seconds and that means right in with the sheep on the hills or close to 'bou on the tundra. Cubs cruise @ 80 or 90 and the M-Four 120, so on headwind days the former move at 50 and I'm at 80+ ground speed. So we get to hike a little further to the game sometimes, but so what? I'm so much faster, have better range and can haul more, a practical thing when supporting Three Eighteens across 1000 miles of this country in my day job.

"OK this is it," I say out loud with a confident voice. Two bull moose are milling in a lake nearby, and I bank and turn low, looking, looking, and there it is! Just a glimpse of a dry creek bed shoots past me where it enters the main river. It's a nice wide gravel fan that looks long enough, except for that snag ending. My hands move quickly now; tanks both, mixture rich, carb heat on, wait … wait … now off, making sure the carb has no ice build on the descent. Gages green I clear the 6 to 2400 rpm and she roars to life, pulling flaps up to full 40 degrees the lever comes up and clicks to the detent under my right armpit. The ship feels like a race horse just before the bell - jerking to life with the power up and ground racing beneath!

I set up flat and level above the trees for another look and pass, and it's mark; ONE, TWO, THREE, FO … the second hand ticks off, "This one's tight with no wind," I say aloud, but once I get on no sweat I think, I'll be going out light and this exit is perfect. (A fly by @ 60mph is about 100 feet-per-second—for example, 3 seconds makes for a 300 foot strip). Full power and the cabin comes to life again, the engine pulling me around with a G right by the moosey lake. They're watching the action out the corner of their eyes now, not stopping to dip for the next mouthful of bottom growth. The lake water is calm. Too bad. I could use a breeze.

I lineup on the gap in the spruce that exposes the fan, seeing the water dripping from the bulls' noses as I race by them, mirrored on the lake and making round ripples around their legs. It seems they're thinking, "this guy's crazy, should be a nice crash today!" They are mostly right—wouldn't be the first time big game in Alaska watched a good wreck!

The approach feels good as the river flashes under me, outside-airspeed-outside-airspeed, but she settles under the big load of gas! FULL POWER!! The ship touches down 3 point and I react; POWER OFF, FLAPS UP, BRAKES, BRAKES!! She bounces hard over the first boulders, bigger than I thought! I roll over a few more to a stop; the snag sits but 30 feet in front of my prop, now swinging away nicely to the softly idling six, like I was parked at International Airport. I'm shaking a bit, so I take a breath and think "OK, I'm here, fuel stash is set!" The tins come out and some go in the wings. I can make it back to the last outpost now, this a perfect spot.

Stepping out on the gravel fan, I pull her around by hand and take a break to look around. I have a funny feeling about this place though, like I'm being watched. This is untouched and wild country, one should never leave the ship without a weapon here. I decide it's better to sightsee with my hunters when I come back in a few weeks, so I jump in, run through the checklist and turn the start switch, she fires up—Ba Bang, Rummmmm. My door is cracked open by habit, "patience," I say to myself. "Ropes off, caps on—fuel—flaps—mixture rich, 2000RPM and mags—left, wait …, right, wait, … then both, and good. Carb heat on … wait, wait ..." I push the lever back in tight. Gages are green. I pull the throttle smoothly back down to 1000. I write the tack time and fuel replaced on my hand in pen.

"Patience, patience, settle down, think, think," I tell myself in another gage scan. "All OK." As I close the door with a flick and look down my boulder runway thinking, "I need to rotate by that root, immediately bank right and visit my friends over the pond … that will work. Brakes on, all good, patience now." Applying full power the engine roars to life. The entire ship is shaking now, held back from rolling by the brakes … ok ready, release … NOW! The ship surges forward responding to the thrust, light now with the fuel tins out—the gear starts pounding over the rocks adding to the din in the cabin and here comes 40!—Rotate! The flap handle comes up under my armpit and the yoke comes back at the same instant. Just as quick the ground rumble from the mains goes silent; she's off and we're over the river in a flash, the cockpit shutter gone, all that's left is the wonderful purr of the big 6, what a great machine I think, this is what you're made to do!

A slight right bank through the gap in the spruce and we're now grabbing sky. Already a hundred feet up, I'm freed from Earth and heading for 80. I clean up the flaps and bank left and south … elated now; racing…racing low across the tundra and the deep caribou trails I think - "this is a blast!" "See you guys later," I muse at the moose. This is what it's all about, what a thrill it is flying in this country, you never get used to it!

7

The ones who run in packs

Hunt Day

My head gets back into the present. The hunters are pulling camp and it's time to look for the 'bou today! There are thousands of them out there somewhere, gathering to make the big move to the wintering grounds and it's my job to find them. Those stragglers we saw yesterday are nothing, the big herds are out there somewhere just like the buffalo; we just have to find them, this is no movie—it's the real deal!

Mick climbs in the passenger seat and finds his belt, we're joking and spirits are high. We grew up doing this stuff with backpack and boats in the Southeast Alaska. Mick was in Anchorage as a youngster when they set the bonfire celebrating Statehood day. His dad taught him to hunt moose before he could drive. A lot happened to us both in those years. The Brown ones are always a factor to deal with in Southeast, the little guys here nothing in comparison the ones where we grew up. They eat a lot of grass here, down there they eat meat, roots and berries. You have to be smarter than them and fast with your weapon, so we always packed in and out in pairs. They don't often attack twosomes, unless it's a spooked sow with cubs. You never pack bloody game out on your own there, ever; we both had seen the results of breaking those rules. We tried to bag our game and get out quick. To us, it was like stealing candy from them: they knew we were there and could do nothing about it: and we laughed about it when we got home, but not until. The two of us were seasoned and tough young men now, knew what we could do and were ready for all the options. We didn't know we were both about to be tested to our limits and more this round.

Mick was always super-prepared, had everything thought out and that was nice. Neither of us needed to mother the other out here. He killed moose as a junior higher in the Yakutat country with his dad, raised at the edge of the wilderness. Mick was the boat and fish guy. He caught thousands of reds in his 20-year career gill-netting Bristol Bay, going on to hold a senior biologist position in charge of none less than the Yukon River in his later years.

The aviation and tech. thing was my deal. It had been a rough but exciting last 2 years for me. Too many crashes and friends lost, fruitless searches and few clean rescues. A thousand hours in a Three Eighteen will teach you a lot out here in the Arctic.

It's not a cutesy animal movie place for sure. Flying and working in minus 40 off the mountains sites, no hangars, bad fuel, ice fog and the furry company waiting for you on the ground, who are no friend of a downed crew I will tell you that. After a crash they would literally come running, and not for petting zoo time. We did thwart them more than once though. That time two big black ones were lying outside each door of a ground looped 185 in minus 57, they waiting for dinner in a Cessna can, lucky deal we showed up. And Audi, the flying swan counter picked up after a crash and his lonely 30 day hike out of the Canning.

After Rick's crash in high school I remember giving up on any possibility of there being a God. Why would He allow *that* to happen? What about Mike, Jeff, the others and then FL66? Doesn't matter anyway now. I'm alive, my machine's running good and thousands of 'bou are *out there.*

For me all that mattered was the laws of physics and human effort, that's what's real, me Vs. nature and the human will make things happen. That's how I dealt with this country and it worked fine for me, a formula I would soon find out worked until today.

I jump in, go through the list and turn the starter as *number one* comes to life with the first rev of the prop. Bang, bang braabump, braabump, braabump, the 6 jumps to life and 1800 rpm. Now back to a thousand for the warm-up. Door is open on my side and it's breezy in the cockpit. Got oil pressure, the smells of 80/87 and leather in the cabin, the shake of the big 6 engine bringing the whole river to life. We are here and alive for sure. The airframe is shuttering, the 6 being 'cammed' up to make power and fly, not sit here idling earth-bound. "Patience, patience girl," I say to myself, taking time to think about my job now, oil checked and covered, ropes clear, fuel caps tight, I work the controls and think, *make sure.*

Three Eighteens have a thousand more parts; a turbine turning at 43,500 rpm, complicated fuel controls, pumps, gear boxes, rotor heads, seals, tail and main blades; a pile of hoses, lines, servos, gages, dials and flight controls; all working together to fly. If you want to stay alive here it all must work perfectly—*all* the time, just like this machine, there's no second chances in the mountains!

"You need some temps to grow before I give you more power girl, it's bad for the top end, valves, rockers and all, they need warm oil spreading everywhere before you get more revs," I think to myself. Having these apart before and knowing helps. We wait in the rumbling cockpit; I drop the flaps to 15, fuel-both, mixture-rich, carb heat on, wait, wait ..., back in and off. Gages green, OK girl, where we're going I need you running perfect today!

Now ready, the throttle goes in and we start rolling to the far end, slow but steady, her real purpose is about to happen. While moving and so I don't nick the prop, I check the mags @ 2000 rpm, left, ...wait, wait, then right ... wait, not too fast, I need to know now, make sure, now *both* and good. Patience, patience! I taxi to the end of the bar, a push of power and rocking the yoke lightens the tail and the ship bumps over the gravel 180 degrees facing the take-off direction, looking down this piece of gravel bar runway. OK, it's time! This not for the faint-hearted, we'll make it or end up a pile of expensive junk at the end. I close my door with a flick and check the lock. "Stop, think again, no

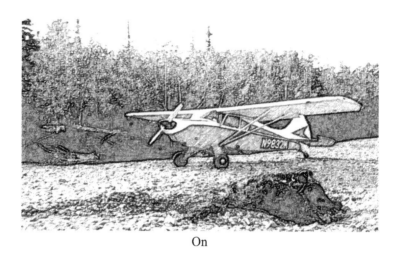

On

hurry, be on top of this," I say to myself. Gages green! Pushing the throttle ball all the way in, the entire airframe is shuttering now, full power! One more scan, oil, fuel, still shuttering ... shuttering ... SHUTTERING, off the brakes—NOW!

The ship surges forward, taking on a life of her own; I just point her down the bar and wait: 100ft ... 200, yoke forward tail up!! 250, this is it! The gear is taking a beating now, the cockpit loud and shaking from the pounding and engine revs. NOW! The flap handle comes up under my armpit, heavy in the prop wash, the same instant back comes the yoke, nose is up and the big mains leave the bar, the RaTaTat from the flinging gravel stops now, and we leap into the air just before touching the river.

The cockpit seemingly goes quiet now, Earth no longer holding us, the bar growing smaller behind as I make a sweeping turn and look back. The solid humming of the 6 still at full power, shouldering all its horsepower into the prop, accelerating us airborne.

Warm air from the cabin heater comforts our senses, the beautiful full power purr dominating the cockpit as we dash higher and faster. Only a little coaxing now, I clean up the flaps and we're gone. "What a wonderful ship!" I think to myself. The river is slipping beneath us with its beautiful turns and sweeps and ribboning before us—so it's easy as she goes and we're outta here. I take a breath, the tension dropping in the cabin and a feeling of accomplishment fills me. We now slip out of sight, a mere dot swallowed in the expanse of the Arctic.

I pull the power back to 2275 and trim for 120Mph as the compass bounces around NE. "Ok, this is good" I think to myself. We're pretty light—just overnight gear, food and rifles, as long as we don't waste fuel, as we will need every drop to find those 'bou and get back to pick up the others. I take a breath thinking it's over for now and settle in for a comfortable ride. We chat happily about the coming day and what lay ahead. It's a perfectly smooth air morning; the big ranges looming up … I think I see a cut—yes, there it is - the Great Canyon the natives told us about! Such features don't show on the maps, you've got to fly the country and get them in your head.

To think that years before these people used to push and pole up this monster with no motor power, can you imagine that! We recall the elder back at the village telling us stories of those times. We enjoyed one of those special evenings when they opened up to us, which was rare. He told us what it was like back then, no snowmachines or fuel oil, just a lot of hard work to feed the sled dogs, gather wood for heating fuel, hunt, fish and survive things that make them close-knit in the villages.

He told us how they poled and dragged up this river, shot their game and came out, a month's long trip, racing against ice-up time. When they got back to the village each family got some meat from their take. Talk about unity and care. I relished what they had.

My parents divorced when I was young, and as the oldest I shouldered a lot of weight for my age. With my adventuresome spirit I learned about the outdoors early and loved it, but was never churched much. I did have a step-gramma that prayed for me and took me to church a few times, but I thought little or never about God, something the older generation did that didn't understand real science and all I mused. My focus was on myself and the excitement of these aircraft, not this religion stuff my friends at school tried to explain to my stubborn heart. I would stop them cold anyway, being so smart and scientific minded you know—the teachers and media did a fine job of that on me. I sometimes wondered how I got out of some bad fixes though, hunting and stuff, but quickly brushed it off as luck.

Sometimes we hiked so far into the mountains we slept in the hides of game we killed. We had s survival mentality. Sleeping in bear country came with its risks too; we slept with our rifles and kept our head back from the end of the tent, when we slept at all. This was our way of living here. Alaska can be a terribly harsh and unforgiving place. Its mountain features extend for hundreds of miles, dwarfing the Alps. Some ascend directly from sea level to over 16,000 feet and higher inland. There are fjords like Norway and plains like the States, all completely uninhabited. Although striking in beauty in winter, while in these elements one sees little of a soft-hearted and kind God, the Bible speaking about a onetime "very good" and pleasant Earth, but it actually can be a harsh and unforgiving place. Life can end in an instant and does for many out here all too often. One place set the record land temperature of minus 87F (that's where we chased the wolves away from a downed 185) and another location that clocked wind speeds of over 250 Mph, the very same area in the Southeast where we grew up, the winds drumming away at the peaks above us and blasting us out of the inland seas as we scampered out for safety. If only our mothers could have seen us! Many didn't make it home. My fingertips had little feeling left in them by the time I was 16, being frozen and thawed so many times. Though never frost bitten myself, I saw its terrible effects. The place certainly made us tough; you never touched the water nor stayed in wet clothes, hyperthermia being an instant killer. We loved our way of life completely but were always mindful of the consequences of a single slipup, those lost to the weather a constant reminder.

The magical complexity of the animal life did perplex me sometimes; their beauty, individualism and personalities seemed thought out. How could this happen by chance? That piece made no sense to me at all. I also knew of the mega-fauna like the mammoths that once lived here; and the lush climate that prevailed in Alaska in times past. What was with that? Trapping I noticed no in-between types, I would look at the anatomy of dozens of animals most folks would never see as a hunter and trapper and this honestly didn't make sense to me either ... though I still bought into the story of evolution. It was "scientific" they claimed and filled our classrooms, books and TV screens.

Today was mild and slightly overcast, without a breath of wind and the ship ran along her path silky-smooth, the cabin unusually calm and quiet. Mick and I became philosophic about the surroundings and all, talking about our past adventures while I idled down to watch for game. While chatting like brothers over the hum of the 6, we came around the corner and broke out of the Great Canyon—a massive plain extended majestically before us. It seemed we had found the Shangri-La of the Brooks Range, the spectacle before us no picture or words could describe. It was one of those experiences of discovery that escapes description, like seeing Mt McKinley or the Grand Canyon for the first time. We had both seen many amazing sights in Alaska, but were aghast at the scene before us. Then it happened.

8

The entire valley is covered with tens of thousands of 'bou - including the landing area's (Image ADF&G)

The Great Arctic Herd is Found

Over the years, I have found that beautiful country often equals finding big game, and so it was here. With the initial shock past and still absorbed in the grandeur of the country, I scanned out to the north and left, where a broad treeless valley swept over the horizon providing passage to the summer grounds of the 100,000 square mile North Slope. It was here a motion caught my eye, but more than a spot of movement; the ground seemed to be moving, refocusing to make sure I wasn't seeing an illusion ... it

Lower Camp

seemed now the *entire plain was moving!* "It's the Arctic Herd!" Mick exclaimed, the spectacle instantly electrifying the cabin. "Wow, have you ever seen anything like it!" - astounded at the scene unfolding before us. No camera lens or canvas could capture it; we were at exactly the right place at exactly the right time to witness this once a year event. This was the Arctic Herd in full motion in its annual move from the summer to winter grounds, all in this setting of abject beauty and wonder, and what an amazing sight it was!

Keeping a wide birth so as not to disrupt the animals, we toured for 20 minutes as they kept coming and coming. On a remote hillside we noticed a group we were sure were bulls, and as we got closer other males among the bands became apparent, but these boys stood out; it was then we came to the realization that these were *monsters*, *the lead bulls of the entire Arctic Herd, watching the grand progression as their wards passed by!* Even lying they stood out, their massive racks sticking up like so many trees in the treeless tundra. Stunned by it all and regaining our thoughts, it was now time to get down to business. Looking south, I saw what looked to be a good landing spot near their path. "This is too good to be true," I thought. I was soon to find out it was.

Upper Camp

Flying over the river bar at 60, I found one end had serious boulders but the other was long and safe, so it was game time. Fuel, mixture, carb heat on ... off ... gages green, 2000 rpm, full flaps, I run through the checklist: a very, very important process when an urgent need to land is imminent, also a time when many a pilot skips a step and pays dearly for it. Then my eye hits the ammeter on the front panel: looking again I see the needle is hard to positive! Darn, I think, must have lost my regulator! Well, no big deal for now, I thought, so I pull that breaker and the needle settles left of center;—safe in discharge mode. Now an aircraft engine doesn't need a battery to run at all—the ignition comes from dual "magnetos" firing 2 spark plugs per cylinder independent of the battery. In its wisdom the FAA required such a safety system for all piston aircraft engines. "I can make it back to lower camp," I thought to myself, "move them up and dash in for parts while these guys have the time of their lives here!" As I circle and lineup, full flaps now—60, 55, 45, power out, flare and set down ... Bang, BaBa Bang, Bang! We roll to a safe but thumpy halt. This is perfect! Mick wouldn't have to move an inch from camp—why pack the meat?

Out of the ship we divide up the survival gear—tent, rifles, knife, fire making and food, I my 243, Mick his 300 so each of us could hold out fine if needed. More than once a pilot has dropped off his hunters then crashed coming out: and no one knew the wiser. As we were sorting this out, oh boy, boldly here comes the herd: they will be crossing the river near here soon! Evening was upon us now, not much time to get back up here; so I jump in, hit the start switch and Rummm! up comes number one. The empty ship moves nimbly now, light on fuel, gear and no Mick aboard. I run my checks, "patience, patience, no time for a stupid mistake," I say. Flaps, fuel, mixture, mags checked left, right and on both, carb heat on, wait … off … wait, off, oil OK, gage group, gen is out, fuel caps on, ropes off, doors secure. I taxi to the far end and sit while the engine idles at 1200, "Well ok," I think, "I will call for weather when I get in range of the RCO (an FAA unmanned radio site used to help bush aircraft to call in) and call in and check the weather into Kotz and talk about options. I wonder if Warren is on tonight, he knows his stuff, flown here since the 50's, even in the same cub! We will be in hand-prop mode to conserve battery, this done often as many bush planes have no generator anyway, but tricky with novice helpers I note.

I look around, throttle goes in and she rotates off the bar in short order. Flaps come up, power back, a wave of my wings at Mick and I disappear down the Great Canyon sprinting along at 140 for base camp. I worked out a marking setup with Mick if I have to land late. All good, or so I thought...

The New Situation

The situation has now changed, I can't depend on these guys to hand prop me for safety reasons, fatal mistakes have been made before from this operation. Looking south I can see the weather is changing, and not for good. I must land, fuel, load gear and client then get to the upper camp before darkness sets in. My outs are good, I have a village strip a few hours out then lower camp, but neither has night lighting. I will wait on the town trip option for now. Maybe stay in the upper country till tomorrow.

The lower landing sandbar of base camp looms up but minutes of precious light are clicking off as dusk comes on. Fuel, flaps, mixture, carb heat on ... off ... gages ... ammeter still stone cold. I clear the engine on the 60mph approach and flash over the river heading direct to the touchdown point—Bang, Ba Bang she sets down nicely in half the length. I taxi up with the good news: we found the 'bou, thousands of them, but better get going. We load and I put on the fuel I need, plenty to get up and back, yet keep the ship light to do this type of close quarters work. I think of another out, all the way to town if needed.

We're both in, my door open so I hit the switch and she comes to life, all is good and light for the trip to upper camp, this is great! I taxi to the end. "Patience, patience," I tell myself, don't get in a hurry—"use your head!" I think; ropes, caps, flaps, fuel, mixture, carb heat, 2000rpm on the back taxi, mags both. Gages; the nagging generator is still out. I pause and clear my mind. "Focus man, patience, slow this down," I say to myself, checklist again. In goes the throttle, 100, 200, 300 feet, I rotate and the ship jumps off, a headwind now! You never get used to it! I cleanup to cruise speed and race north for the ending of this day. I make the call, the experienced FAA man from the area comes on the air. I explain my generator issue and the idea of coming in tonight. "Fine," he says, "come on in, weather's fine all the way." My option list is growing, that's good news! Or so I thought …

9

A bull watches (Image ADF&G)

Too Many 'Bou

We tack up the Big Canyon and the big open plain soon appears, my passenger taken aback at what lay before us in the fading light. The 'bou are now stretched along the river, thousands of them, all the way back to the horizon. I figure, "no problem, Mick will have the strip cleared even if he has to shoot them off," but it was not to be. Looking out as we approached, I see the whole bar moving, Mick is in the corner with tent up waving his hands in exasperation, so I circle and try to get my head around the situation. We have too many 'bou here and light is failing! They have covered all the landing options up and down the canyon!

I try to try buzz them away—no deal, all I can do is circle and circle as the light fades, all those big bulls waving their racks in disgust as if saying, "You're in our way here, this is our country!" This situation has now changed for the worse as I watch the fuel needles bouncing off "E." "Come on, get outta the way!" I say out loud, and finally they start to thin out, only as this party crosses the river. Mick has setup the markers as planned, but it's all a grey/black mass in the fading dusk now, river, gravel and boulders. So I setup for landing. The red panel lights in the cockpit are on now, it's near past dusk and the landing light comes on with the last of the battery.

Disaster Looms

I line up on the bar flying west into the last glimmer of light for reference, but the markers are not on my side now, they're on the passenger's because the wind changed. I ask him to call off when he sees them go by, "ok, got it," he says. Good, I think, "a few more seconds and this day will finally be over."

Beyond those markers are boulders and then a canyon, big enough to take my gear off or worse. I must be right on … fuel, flaps mixture, carb heat on … off … gages green, 2000 rpm and 60, now 60, and over the river we flash, now comes the bar, wait, wait, I get ready and hear "NOW!" I chop power but something's wrong, at the same instant it happens, Bang, Ba Bang, BANG!—I must be LONG!

All at once I decide to bale out of this deal - Full Power and Nose up as my mains clear the beginning of the end. We're airborne, but something odd has happened: my rudder is acting funny. "Oh man!" I think, "I did it now!" The tail wheel is severed and dangling back there, held only by the cables! It's kicking the rudder around wildly! "Come on, break loose! BREAK LOOSE!" After what seems an eternity it breaks away. By design the manufacturer installed aluminum safety clips that snap away in cases like this, allowing me to regain full control of my rudder, as the tail wheel gets a one-way trip into the canyon with no parachute. Lucky for us we're not along for that ride! The passenger had called off the marker too late, I had landed in the red zone. I had taken a chance, pushed my limits and nearly lost the ship, or worse.

I turn back to check on Mick. He's OK, and knows were done for the night. We open the side hatch and kick out extra gear for him on the fly and wave goodbye. He's not sure he will ever see us again, being it's snowing and knowing we can't try again in the dark. Now we are in a fix; I have a gen failure and a lost tail wheel, so I can't land on the gravel tonight! I need good weather now to make it into the village. The positive side is that I do have a dual power instrument panel and know how to use it—thanks to my check ride last summer. 1/2 the critical flight instruments are on a vacuum system not needing a battery, so that's good. Bad news is I will really have to conserve fuel, but all is still OK: weather is good back to Kotz, the man said, so I can make a direct run in as long as we don't have any further complications. But I have a bad feeling in my gut now, I have zero outs. Darn caribou.

As I round the corner of the Great Canyon, I don't like what I see; it looks like weather has filled the whole lower country behind me in an hour! How is that! I dial up the RCO and make the call, "Flight service this is 98M, xxx miles off the xxxx RCO." Almost instantly, a familiar voice comes back over the air. Man does he sound good tonight!

10

A Brown One

The Last Leg

"Sorry about this change in weather, no one saw it coming!" I explain my situation giving him Mick's location and details. Flying direct into Kotz is my only option now, hold a course down river and look for a break to conserve fuel, my precious gas stash worthless in the stormy dark night. Wow, this trip is a long way from over. I've got to think, think! It's like a chess game all gone wrong, thinking one had their opponent cornered then in a flurry of moves you're in check and lost your queen to boot! "Man oh man; this is not good," I think, "not good at all!" I going over every option possible and coming up with nothing. I hate what I see on those gas gages. It wears on you - the time on my palm agrees: I've got much more flight time to go than fuel.

As I was negotiating the situation from 1000 feet heading south, Mick was on the ground hundreds of miles from nowhere with his hands full. The first thing you do when you're stuck in the bush is to assess the situation. Where to set up for the night in a safe place for one (no simple task when surrounded by thousands of square miles of nothing but plains, rivers, mountains and lots of hungry carnivores with teeth). You have to pick a protected and defendable spot when on your own with only a few ounces of tent fabric between you and them. Around this river was nothing but open ground, deep creek cuts, brush mounds and open flats. It was also home to many animals with a perfect sense of smell and no one is off the menu, as most the big predators have little fear of man here. What goes on after dark can be terrifying at times, and what happens on the heels of the Arctic Herd even worse. But Mick thinks he has no choice—the river bar is the safest place to be. He sets up the tent just off the thousand-year path of the entire Western Arctic Herd. Mick's in for a stay of his life.

Next, he takes stock of his provisions. On the last flyby we kicked out my Arctic coverall suit, check; tent is OK, 300Mag rifle ammunition, three in my gun and now, let's see, where are they? Opening every package, pouch and bag, he finally finds the precious yellow waterproof ammo box, but to his horror he opens it and what does he find? A 20 round lineup of nice *243 Winchesters* for MARK'S GUN!! He can't believe his eyes. Fine, great, of all the times not to have ammo, he thinks, I will just hold off the entire Arctic Herd, the Browns, the packs, wolverines and everything else with my knife and *THREE ROUNDS!*

Mick was left with three rounds

Least Mick always carried a really big army knife … ever since school we joked with him about it. But now it was no joke, as mounted on a tent pole of stick he actually had a very formidable weapon, one any Eskimo of olden days would use with confidence, except on the big brown ones, and they were everywhere here.

Now his situation was very serious, there was no safe place to make an escape. If you left they smelled you out on a night trail. If you stayed put all these guys that trailed the herd would be on to you. He just hoped I had got a call off and someone would come through and pick him up. "I'm sure they will send someone tomorrow," he told himself. "I can hold out fine with 3 rounds." But then it started to snow and the weather closed down; and tomorrow's pickup never came. You see the Arctic has a mind of its own, and no one had any idea he had only three rounds to his name.

Pitching his tent on part of the bar where the 'bou passed in the least numbers turned out a failure: a traffic jam is a traffic jam, as we had unknowingly picked *the* ancient river ford used by this herd for *centuries!* Day and night thousands upon thousands passed by, around, and nearly over his tent, and Mick did use one round of his precious ammo as a last resort; fresh meat and a hide to sit on was comforting.

Between the crossings the worst time was at night; that's when the predators that follow the herds came boldly, but a fire and yelling did the trick warding off those, making for a long night on guard duty. Sitting in front of the tent in the coverall suit we dropped, Mick thought— "least Mark did something right," not knowing it was against the overtures of the selfish passenger that he got the suit at all. Cat napping between crossings during the day, this guest of the Arctic got all the caribou viewing he could stand and more, a true Alaska 5 star vacation. But Mick is smart, tough, experienced and confident; he knew he would be OK. He was mostly worried sick about us. Mick's mom was always a little wary of me, if she could only see the mess I had got Mick into now!

As I set a course for Kotz, I could see that something was very wrong out ahead. Soon the ceiling was dropping fast; and in a few more miles it was solid to the ground. Worse yet, as I was being forced lower and lower, I couldn't take a direct route but wound up following the ribbon like winding river, doubling my flight time. I ran the calcs in my head over and over and I couldn't believe it! I now didn't have the gas to make it in! This headwind, gen out, partial panel and all that precious fuel sitting there untouchable in the night! The weather now covered my alternate and visibility turned to zero. Staying put sleeping on the rocks with Mick now sounded awfully good! I should have circled back and landed. Too late for that now, I was stuck in the air!

The realities were now hitting home, with so much planning and an out, how in the world could such a trap have sprung on me? In those days we had no weather radar, satellites and such; the deal was Kotzebue was clear for miles but this fall system had rushed in between us! I had gotten out of jams like this before but this one had a different twist: low fuel, tail wheel plus the gen failure. I got to thinking about some of the S&R's I had been on, looking for really experienced pilots in good aircraft—inexplicably lost. I don't like this one, I don't want to end up like them; "there must be some way out of this" I thought. At this point I radioed in I was going IFR, (on complete instruments) so I climbed to clear the mountain range out front on partial panel, but the fuel issue, the fuel! It was the life or death factor now. I leaned the mixture to maximum and set up for best economy. My calcs told me otherwise, we needed 8 more gallons. I had never been wrong before at the pumps, I knew this machine well and now it was likely to be my coffin!

I started thinking about the headlines. Man, what an idiot! Should get a medal for this! Few would care—my parents, a few friends, the guys at work. "Told you he always pushed the limits too far," our chief pilot would say. "Pretty low time for that kind of work," one of my past enemies would bark. Were they right and I wrong? Sure looks like it tonight. The announcement script that would run on the station's went through my head, a too often story line in Alaska. That last time they thought I had bought it in the Nabesna country, but I fooled them! Capt. Anderson got me out thanks to Doug Fredrick's. Was minus 30 but I had the basic equipment and made fires, and the packs couldn't find me till the last night, but too bad, I got out! They ran the lost report for 10 days before word got back home I was safe. They were taking food to my mom, except for Pat; he told them all, "he's tough and smart, he'll make it out"—and I did! I was always grateful for Pat's confidence in me after that. They told me the year before a guy in the same fix was never seen again, not even a piece of clothing was found. Yeah, the packs got him for sure, but not me.

The question that perplexed me was why now? I'm out here doing the same thing as the other guys, who ever heard of all this stuff ganging up on a guy like this tonight in one flight? And why me ... now? Then it hit me—the instructor in Fairbanks; he would tell us over and over, "It's not just one thing but a number of factors that stack up that kills a good crew." The more I thought about his comments the worse this looked. Was my number up? Is this how it was for all the others?

To think how this day started so well and now here I am in this fix, about to kill myself and an innocent passenger to boot! He's getting restless and sees the fuel gages on "E." My mind calculated and strategized in frustration over and over: who in the world, what can I do about this? What other strips, flat areas? Nothing! I could come up with *nothing!* Everything is socked in but Kotz, I must go for Kotz! I thought of Audi flying from Kaktovic to town with a friend and a load of laundry, then number 1 engine quits on top ("on top" means you're flying in the clear above the clouds, but a mountain range is in the mist below you). "At least that was *day*," I thought. I remember he tells her to shout if she sees ground; all of a sudden she screams, he flairs the machine and bam! Impact! It took 10 days to find them, both lived but spent months recovering from injuries. Walt was smart enough to risk it during the day, but not me, invincible me ... I can't pull that one off at night, no one has got out of a deal like this and lived to tell about it.

"Were going to crash, aren't we?" the passenger exclaims. "I hate the nervous types," I think to myself. We're in a full blizzard now. We have battery left, though, my navigation equipment has Kotz locked in and the engine is running smooth, for now ... But wait for that to end in a few minutes. Then it starts to happen. I hear a miss. I think back in time, wondering what Rick was thinking when he got into that fix with a family aboard. Now I know how he felt; it's a feeling of complete helplessness, you resign yourself to the inevitable; man at the end of himself with no answers. This must be it for me, I thought, but why had I escaped those other times, why not now?

All of a sudden it hit me: what if there *is* a God? What if Mr. Science wise guy here had it all wrong and Gramma was right? Well, if ever there was a time ... I really don't want to die, and this is totally unfair to my passenger, to heck with me! I thought I felt the engine miss again. "So this is what it's like," I thought, then waited for Big 6 to go silent.

So many conflicts and no answers here, but why have all those innocent people I knew and flew with died? Then it hit me: what if I ask? It wasn't in the training; not a section for this in my little orange FAA Alaska Supplement, there was lots of good info in there, even a section about what to do if a Mig jumped you ... Then it just came out—in my mind I spoke these words and meant them—

"If there's a God, I need your help, now!"

At that very moment a light came into the cockpit and in my mind, and a clear male voice said;

"Son, you said the right thing!"

Just like that. All of a sudden the engine smoothed u... and in a few moments we sprung out of the snowstorm! And there, like a wonderful dream, what was in my wind-screen?—*the lights of Kotzebue*, the beautiful lights of Kotz it was, like the Celestial City itself, all lit up on the horizon and *dead ahead!* We actually have a chance now I thought. There was only one minor problem left: you see, we were over deadly cold water now, 8 minutes to cross on two empty tanks, but after that little chat I expected to make it across—and we did, thank *God.*

As I lined up on the west runway of Kotzebue, Alaska, there was a different guy at the controls now. I wasn't nearly so proud thinking *I* was in control. I setup to land; fuel (ha!), flaps, mixture, carb heat on … off … Power up! Gage scan, altitude, airspeed, altitude, airspeed, wings level, descent at a few hundred, 60 mph, 60, 60, level, level, easy and…down! The mains are on and the wheels are turning on the runway. What a sweet sound the pavement made on those turning wheels!

Tying down that night, I thought about who or what had spoken to me. This is a shock of shocks! All the times I had rebuffed my believing friends, took lightly the whole God and Church thing: and the language … Mr. Hotshot know it all here was a pretty guy humble now. When I got back to town there would be no more mocking God for me.

Warren and May going home…

Epilogue

Warren flew out to check on Mick when the weather broke five days later, finding him calm and OK, gave him an update and some food. I fixed the ship and flew back out finding him standing there looking a little crusty, weapon nearby and his army knife on stick. "Very period Mick" I said. He wasn't in a laughing mood.

We went on and shot some real nice 'bou. My hunt experience was interesting; A nice herd of about 250 surrounded me while I hid on the ground, afraid to shoot for fear of being trampled. Upon being discovered the herd froze so I pulled the trigger on a nice one and stood up quickly. Unknowingly I had pinged the lead bull, the herd then halting to pick a new leader, which took about 20 minutes. In this I got to watch a very interesting process while they mourned the lost then re-gathered to move on. Such is life I thought.

Warren asked me to make a fuel run up to their cabin and May Thomson, Warren's wife, invited me in for some chicken soup. I thought she meant Campbell's, so at first declined, not wanting to impose. I flew in another load and she persisted. When they opened that cabin door I couldn't believe my eyes; there was a *whole chicken* covered in big noodles overflowing the pot, wow! I feasted like a wolf and thought, "this married life must not be so bad!" Things were changing for me fast and in a good way. Later more was in store for me from this voice that called me "Son" that night. We said our goodbye's and flew home, never to see them again. It was then the country was divided. I never went back.

The next year I read the entire Bible cover to cover on a bet from a girl. I came to embrace God as a fair, good and understanding guy but still held onto life's steering wheel, and not doing a very good job of it myself. Then one of my Three Eighteens crashed and my life was spared again; and on the extraction flight out in a place far away, I decided that God's Son, Jesus Christ, was the true Way, so I gave my life and foolish beliefs away in the back cabin of a Twin Otter over the Yukon River. I began to look seriously at why I had believed the things I did about origins and science, and the Lord opened my eyes showing me in part why all the harshness, evil and pain existed in this world, one thing being sure: that this dispensation will end someday and things will be restored like new. That it all was once a "very good" world made for man to enjoy and the game to thrive in. I now understood that life is a gift and we live in vital times. I started speaking and teaching about creation and the "very good" world that then was, and was later destroyed: and that today we see only a remnant of the original, like the harshness of Alaska and the heartbreak in this world. It all began to make more sense.

I carried around the fuel slip showing the fillup after that night for many years; it read 40.8 gals out of the 38 that that aircraft can hold full. I never turned back, that was 6 children and 38 years ago.

I should note that due to good management by the Alaska Department of Fish and Game there are more than 5 times as many 'bou in the Arctic now, so you can still view and harvest them across the thousands of square miles of Alaska, and maybe someday be a *Long Hunter* yourself!

Mick is now Senior Biologist for ADF&G's Yukon River Fish program and doing a fine job, always advocating for better conditions and medical care in the villages, speaking the native tongue and helping to sustain the salmon runs so critical to so many in Alaska. He survived other crashes among the Browns and packs over the years, yet always seems to make it home in one piece! May Thompson went on to be with the Lord in June of 2013. I know she's in Heaven now and would want you to know this story. Warren Thompson is now retired with over 35,000 safe flying hours and many, many rescues to his credit. He's still sharp as a tack enjoying his children, grandchildren and his Alaska. God Bless them all, someday we will all be together again, flying and watching the big herds on the move!

Kenneth Patrick Millard passed away in September, 1982 at the age of 30. He was doing what he loved best - being at sea. Our last conversations were about knowing God.

As for me I changed careers a few times. For a while I took care of navigation electronics on heavy jets. One night I noticed the ground based guidance equipment at the airport was out, but the tower guys said it was green on their screen. I had no peace about it: I double checked, and as it turned out, I was right. There were heavies inbound that night. Maybe that's one reason I lived, God only knows. Our life here is like bugs in a pond bottom compared to heaven. Where He lives is a much finer place. This is a University.

I will be the first to tell you I don't have all the answers. I do know one thing: your reading this story right now is no accident, and I was spared for a reason and maybe you are it. Please take heed and seek the God I found through the Bible and heard from that night. If he touched a proud sinner like me, he has the same gift and favor for you right now! He is not so High and Mighty of heart that you are meaningless to Him. He came among us as a man to prove this, but they killed Him, the Son of Creation itself and as such He became the true expression of love we can all trust. He understands our predicament, like that night when I had no outs and no answers, no reason in the world to be worthy of saving, He came through for me. He will come through for you too in any trouble you have, ready to show Himself powerful on your behalf as he did for this kid, even to the very end. This promise is for all who believe, being kept for the day of redemption, either at the point of death or when He returns. This life is not the end of itself, its temporary; a new world is to come! Search these things out and see if the words of the Bible speak to you in these matters, that's all good with God too. Jesus said, "I Am the Way, The Truth and the Life, no man comes to the Father except through Me," and He cannot lie. It's a good deal, take care of your soul and spirit – its eternal!

God Bless you in your quest for truth, and may you find peace with Him! Before that night I was certain there were only three absolutes in life: matter, physics and human effort. I was dead wrong, there's a fourth element above all: Almighty God!

Another Title by Mark Rose

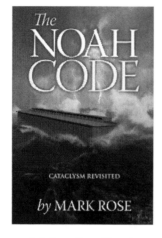

This new book takes off on Alaska where Long Hunters leaves off. Explaining the beautiful *First Earth* as made by the Creator "in the beginning" and after, this volume may be the most important work on the Flood and creation accounts written in 60 years. *The Noah Code* expounds on the first chapters of Genesis from a new and fresh perspective, referencing hundreds of sources new and lost for centuries in the research of the author, explaining the Flood catastrophe, mountain formation, Flood traditions, mega-fossil deposits and geology from the best and latest sources both old and new. Over 330 pages packed with 110 illustrations, custom maps and charts, this work will prove to be a classic on this important topic.

Order today direct and learn more on this critical topic:
www.noahcode.org
Kindle

Comments: info@genesisalive.com

What others are saying about The Noah Code—

"Mark Rose has produced a fascinating study of the geologic and other scientific evidence supporting the Biblical account of the Flood of Noah. Anyone with a serious interest in Genesis or the plethora of Flood stories should consider this book."

- Dr. Mark Barclift

"I edit and write reviews for many Christian books and I can honestly say that what you have written goes far and beyond anything I've ever read. It's as if you have left no stone uncovered. I truly believe that God is going to use this book to His glory and as a blessing to multitudes of people."

- Brenda, CBM Reviews "10 Stars"

"Just finished your book and what an excellent job you've done. There are so many Christians who do not believe in the Flood because they don't have the facts ... I deeply appreciate your research which enlightened and informed me one fact after another. I am sure I will be referring back to your book in my own defense of the Flood of Noah. I have highly recommended it to a few friends already. Thanks again Mark..."

- Allen Austin, author, *Genesis in Egypt*

Next in series coming in 2016!
Don't miss out on the next in series of the Long Hunter saga— **Last of the Long Hunters II.** This title will focus on the helicopter in Alaska, the author teaming with some of Alaska's greatest bush helicopter pilots. Don't miss out on this coming thriller. Printing scheduled for March of 2016

Mark Rose worked professionally in Alaska aviation for many years. He later traveled the world working in some of the deepest underground mines of all types. His experiences there and in Alaska convinced him that the crust of the Earth had gone through a revolution that aligns fully with the Biblical account of Noah's Flood.